Stories of Saints
and the Beatitudes

Stories of Saints and the Beatitudes

Marie Paul Curley, FSP, and Mary Lea Hill, FSP

With a Foreword by
Deacon Pedro Guevara-Mann

Pauline
BOOKS & MEDIA
BOSTON

Library of Congress Control Number: 2025941997

ISBN 10: 0-8198-1702-3

ISBN 13: 978-0-8198-1702-0

Cover art/design and interior art by www.knjms.com

Published by Pauline Books & Media, 50 Saint Paul's Avenue, Boston, MA 02130-3491

Printed in the U.S.A.

www.pauline.org

Pauline Books & Media is the publishing house of the Daughters of St. Paul, an international congregation of women religious serving the Church with the communications media.

1 2 3 4 5 6 7 8 9   31 30 29 28 27 26

For our mothers,
Alvada L. Hill
and
Mary Teresa Curley,
who taught us with their lives and their love
how to live the Beatitudes

Contents

BLESSED ARE THOSE WHO ARE PERSECUTED
FOR RIGHTEOUSNESS' SAKE, FOR THEIRS IS
THE KINGDOM OF HEAVEN.

Foreword

"We are all called to be saints." I first heard this expression when I was on the organizing committee for World Youth Day 2002. Don't get me wrong. I had been in the Church all my life—sacraments, catechism, CCD, youth group, music ministry, retreats, and young adult groups—but never heard anyone say anything about the "universal call to holiness." And yet there we were, planning the biggest Catholic event in the world while making sure our guiding principle would be to provide a positive experience of the Church for the young people in order to help them get to heaven. That's the mission of the Church. That's why we "go . . . make disciples of all nations" (Mt 28:19).

Yet, were I to ask you who are reading this if you want to be a saint, how would you answer? Would you think that you are not "saint material"? Would you think that you are not "holy enough"? But what is a saint? Basically, a saint is someone who is in heaven, right? By this definition, if you desire heaven, then you should want to be a saint.

Because, after all, nothing else matters: getting to heaven—that's the goal. My friend, singer/songwriter Steve Angrisano (whom I met while planning WYD 2002), loves to tell audiences during his concerts that heaven is the only option. Then he adds, "Well, there is another option, but it's not a good one. Heaven. Let's stick to plan A."

We are created for heaven.

Most of us will not be officially recognized (or canonized) as saints. My mother was a good and holy woman who strove to live every day of her life in accordance with God's word. I am confident that she is in heaven. She may never be recognized as a saint. But that doesn't mean that she isn't in heaven. In my mind, she is a saint; she's just not canonized.

When the Church canonizes someone (as I learned while working for WYD), it isn't just a guarantee that this person is in heaven; the Church is also giving us a role model who can guide us in our attempts to live a holy life. That is why every World Youth Day has patron saints. I still remember the ones from 2002: Blessed Pier Giorgio Frassati, Blessed Pedro Calungsod, and Blessed Kateri Tekakwitha (all of whom have since been canonized), as well as Saint Agnes of Rome, Blessed Andrew of Phu Yeng, Saint Josephine Bakhita, Saint Thérèse of Lisieux, Blessed Francisco Castelló Aleu, and Blessed Marcel Callo. Of these, I had only ever heard of Saint Thérèse and Saint Agnes. Now they are all part of my team in heaven: a group of young people to whom I can relate, who had the same desires and struggles as I did, and who tried, every day, to put God first and do his will in their lives. (If you haven't heard of some of them, read on to meet a few!)

Since then, I have been a cheerleader for the saints. I've stolen Steve Angrisano's line and use it as much as I can ("Really, there is no other option"). I share as many stories of saints as I can with as many people as I can and I have become more aware of how much the Church celebrates our saints by observing memorials and special feast days.

Along the way, it dawned on me that when Jesus tells his disciples in the Gospel of Matthew that blessed are the poor in spirit . . . the meek, those who mourn . . . the pure of heart . . . the merciful and peacemakers, those who hunger for righteousness and who suffer persecution for his sake (see Mt. 5:3–10), he is giving us a map of how to be blessed; how to be holy; how to be saints. The Beatitudes are a guide to sainthood. It's no coincidence that this is the Gospel reading on the Solemnity of All Saints.

When I learned that my dear friend, Sister Marie Paul Curley, FSP, and the "Crabby Mystic," Sister Mary Lea Hill, FSP, were compiling a book and connecting stories of saints to the Beatitudes, I had to get my hands on it. It is a beautiful trip around the world representing the universality of the Church. It is also a practical guide to living our faith. Saints are good role models and they teach us about the faith, but often it's not easy to see how their lives are connected with specific tenets of the faith. *Stories of Saints and the Beatitudes* shares exciting stories of real people which show that living the Beatitudes is possible and that we, too, can be saints who proclaim our faith through our ordinary day-to-day living.

This new edition has been updated with extra details and resources so that the saints' lives are even more accessible to you, with fun facts, quotes, prayers, questions for reflection, and saintly challenges. I know you've likely heard of Francis of Assisi,

Juan Diego, Bernadette, Catherine of Siena, Frances Cabrini, Gregory the Great, Elizabeth of Hungary, and Monica. But I bet you've never thought of them the way they are presented in this book. Earlier I mentioned Tekakwitha and Pier Giorgio; perhaps you didn't know them yet. In the pages that follow, you will get to know them better. Maybe you also haven't yet heard of Germaine Cousin, Teresita de Quevedo, Martin de Porres, Marie-Clémentine Anuarite, Isidore Bakanja, and Mary MacKillop. Except for Martin de Porres, a few years ago, I hadn't either. They are all now part of my team in heaven. After you read their stories, I promise that you will be inspired, and they will become part of your team too! I also promise that thanks to these stories, the Beatitudes will come to life for you. You will never again hear the words of Jesus inviting us to be "blessed" without thinking of these sixteen saints.

The theme for WYD 2002 was from Matthew 5:13–14: "You are the salt of the earth; you are the light of the world." These are the words that Jesus speaks immediately after he teaches the Beatitudes to the crowds sitting on the mount. Being the salt of the earth and light of the world is directly related to being blessed. But Jesus doesn't say, "You are *called* to be salt of the earth" or "you are *called* to be light of the world." He says, "You are . . ."

We are not merely "called" to be saints. We are created for sainthood. It is not an option. The only option is to say "yes" to whom we are meant to be. May the lives of these sixteen "blesseds" inspire you to say "yes" to whom God is forming you to be. May they also inspire you to be poor in spirit, pure of heart and meek, to hunger for righteousness and be merciful, to be peacemakers and yes, to also be persecuted and to mourn—we are in good company! It is the company of saints in heaven, where we, too, one day hope to be.

Deacon Pedro Guevara-Mann

June 13, 2025 (Feast of Saint Anthony of Padua)

BLESSED ARE THE POOR
IN SPIRIT, FOR THEIRS IS
THE KINGDOM OF HEAVEN.

Saint Francis of Assisi

Holy Fool

Born: c. 1182 in Assisi
Died: October 3, 1226, just outside Assisi (at the Portiuncula)
Feast Day: October 4
Canonized: 1228 by Pope Gregory IX
Patron: Italy and the environment

Francis saw his father Pietro frown at him as he walked in the front door of the textile business. Francis didn't even stop to greet his mother but walked right past both parents into the back storage room.

He could hear his father sputtering to his mother as he continued folding and piling the material from the new shipment. "I don't understand him! He joins the duke's army . . . a splendid knight . . . he had the whole town in the palm of his hand. And in two days—*two days*, mind you—he slinks back home, a disgrace to the Bernardone name! He's a fool!"

His mother's soft voice trembled. "I don't pretend to understand him, but you know he hasn't been himself since he came back. Maybe he just needs time to find his way."

In the next room, Francis cringed. He had decided to join the duke's army to reclaim the glory he had lost languishing as a prisoner of war. But something hadn't felt right. Then he'd heard that voice, that compelling voice too demanding to ignore: "Serve the Master, rather than man." He could still hear it ringing in his ears. Coming back had made him seem a cowardly fool, but he couldn't help it.

Francis had never experienced anything like this before. He was used to being the carefree merrymaker, the life of every party. But that sort of tinsel held no more appeal for him. He yearned for something deeper, more real—but what? He slid off the pile of material on which he had been perched. "Mamma, I'm going out to Saint Damian's," Francis called over his shoulder as he strode out the door. His father just shook his head, folding and piling more furiously.

As Francis walked through the winding streets toward the city walls, he was hardly aware of anything around him. Hands stuffed in his belt and head hunched forward, he worked his mind hard. *I can't just keep drifting*, Francis thought. *What am I really looking for? Had that voice belonged to God? How can I "serve the Master"?*

Francis was already outside the city walls and nearly at Saint Damian's Church when a shadow fell across the path, startling him out of his reverie. Instinctively he pulled back in horror as a leper extended his trembling, rotted hand, pleading for coins. From the purse at his belt, Francis drew a few coins and threw them at the human wreck. As the leper struggled to retrieve the coins, Francis circled widely around him and tried to settle back into his interrupted thoughts. Sights like this always left him a little queasy, and he shook his head to clear it. Now, where had he been . . . oh, yes, he had been thinking of how to serve the Master . . .

Francis stopped dead in his tracks. His stomach tightened in a knot of realization and remorse, and he spun around in time to see the leper shuffling around a bend in the road. "Wait!" he shouted hoarsely, breaking into a dead run. He caught up with the man. Panting, torn between desire and revulsion, Francis gripped those thin, ragged shoulders and looked searchingly into the surprised leper's face. Before, he had seen only the ugliness of disease; now he marveled at the light that appeared in the leper's eyes. Francis embraced the leper energetically, as if he were a long-lost friend instead of a man dying of a repulsive, contagious disease. Quickly, simply, Francis emptied the entire contents of his purse into the leper's hand—not throwing the coins but pressing them warmly into the filthy palm. Then, without a word, he turned back and walked on briskly to Saint Damian's. Francis thought to himself: *This is where I'll find my Master, not only in prayer but also in suffering, and in those who are rejected.*

Kneeling before the altar of the little, dilapidated stone church, Francis contemplated the large crucifix. His searching eyes studied the twisted, agonized face. *This* was the face he had seen reflected in the eyes of the leper. It would be in serving others—whether poor or rich, simple or wise—that he would serve his God. But *how?* He still looked for something more concrete that he could do.

As he continued praying, Francis thought he heard someone calling him. Startled, he glanced around, but no one was there, nothing stirred. Yet as soon as he had settled down again, a voice repeated his name: "Francis!" The voice came from the crucifix! "Restore my church, Francis, which is falling into ruins." Francis nodded. This was something he could do—Saint Damian's could use more than a little fixing up.

Francis returned to his father's shop, loaded some of the best brocades and silks on a packhorse, and carted them off to nearby Foligno, where he sold everything—even the horse. He went back to Saint Damian's and offered the money to the pastor. Guessing where the money had come from, the priest hesitated to accept it, so Francis left the bag of coins on a windowsill of the church. When Pietro Bernardone learned what his son had done, his long-seething temper exploded. He physically hauled his son before the bishop to demand his money back.

As his father raged on with his public accusations, Francis realized that his anger was not about the money—after all, his father had indulged Francis all his life with fine clothes, food, and luxuries. His father only wanted to stop Francis from his new way of life. It was time for Francis to choose—even though he didn't feel ready, even though he didn't know exactly what he was supposed to do. If he *really* wanted to follow the way of the servant, suffering Christ, then he must put aside everything else. He must rebel against mediocrity.

Francis squared his shoulders and turned to the bishop. "Your Excellency," he began, "I'll return not only his money but even his clothes." So saying, he removed everything he was wearing and added, "Pietro Bernardone is no longer my father; I give everything back to him. From now on I shall say to God, 'Our Father, who art in heaven. . . .'" The bishop was deeply moved. He covered the shivering Francis with his own robe, later giving him an old gardener's tunic to wear. A furious Pietro Bernardone gathered the clothes and money and left Francis there. From then on, Francis would have to rely completely on the providence of God, having nothing to call his own.

Francis dedicated himself completely to the Lord's service. He divided his time between helping at a refuge for lepers and rebuilding the crumbling church of Saint Damian. At first, he was the laughingstock of the town, but as he persevered in his determination to radically live Gospel poverty, the laughter began to lessen.

With the bishop's permission, he began preaching simple sermons to the townspeople. Before long, his Gospel lifestyle and irrepressible joy began to attract others who were dissatisfied with their lives. When Francis and his followers numbered a dozen, he decided it was time to ask the Church to recognize this order that was forming almost spontaneously around him. Together the poor men set out for Rome to seek an audience with Pope Innocent III.

When the dusty, tattered man from Assisi entered the Pope's audience hall, Innocent gasped. The Pope had seen this very man in his dream the night before: Francis had been holding up the crumbling wall of the Lateran Basilica. Surely God must have something great in store for this unknown servant!

With the Pope's full approval, the little group returned to the vicinity of Francis' hometown. They lived in a borrowed stable until they outgrew it. Then a chapel, Our Lady of the Angels, was lent to Francis by a Benedictine abbot, and the growing community built rugged shacks around it for shelter. This tiny church was called the Portiuncula, or "little portion," and was always Francis' favorite, even years later when his friars had spread all over Italy.

Francis guided his men along the simple lines of the Gospel—prayer, poverty, work, and preaching. As he gradually realized that his new order would "build the Church"—not physically but through spiritual renewal—Francis gave himself to preaching tirelessly. He alternated his preaching with times of retreat from the world, either by himself or with a few companions, dedicating himself to prayer and contemplation. Despite his many sufferings, the lighthearted cheerfulness for which he had been known as a youth blossomed into a deep, persistent joy. He would often sing his now-famous Canticle of the Sun: "Praised be my Lord for Brother Sun . . . for Sister Moon, for Mother Earth, for fruits, flowers, grass, for Sister Death. . . ."

Francis' biggest concern was that his followers—who numbered in the thousands—would remain faithful to a life of poverty, service, and obedience. Only fifteen years after the Pope's approval, Francis' health began to fail. When a doctor told him death was near, he exclaimed, "Welcome, Sister Death!" because he knew he would soon see the Lord of his canticle, face to face.

Francis asked to be taken back to the Portiuncula, and a sorrowful procession wound its way out of Assisi and began climbing a small hill. Francis motioned to the brothers to stop. Slowly, painfully, he raised himself on the stretcher, breathing hard from the effort. As the stretcher was lifted once more, he begged his brothers to sing the canticle with him, for him. Their voices quivering with emotion, they began the song so loved by their spiritual father.

Francis lay for a week in a hut at Portiuncula. Toward evening on a day early in October, Francis asked to be brought into the chapel itself and laid on the floor. He joined his whispered voice to those of the friars singing his favorite song of praise to God. The last verse died away; Francis intoned Psalm 141 and then fell silent.

As darkness shrouded the chapel, the forty-four-year-old holy fool of Assisi entered the eternal light of the Master he had so faithfully served.

Personal Challenge

What is one way that I, like Saint Francis of Assisi, can embrace the joy of a free and uncluttered life so that I might find joy in the freedom of following Christ more completely?

Prayer

Saint Francis of Assisi, you radically lived the beatitude "Blessed are the poor in spirit, for theirs is the kingdom of heaven." In a material-istic age that pressures us to focus on possessions as a means of happiness, help us to discover the true joys of following Christ: the joy of service, the joy of a free heart and uncluttered life, the joy of living in reconciliation, the joy of living in communion with all creation. Give us the courage to live in always greater freedom as your instru-ments of Christ's joy and peace in the world. Amen.

Facts About His Life:

~::~ One of the most beloved and popular saints, Francis' feast day is celebrated not just by Catholics but also by the Church of England, the Episcopal Church in the USA, and others.

~::~ Known as the "holy fool," Francis sought out opportunities to be ridiculed.

~::~ Just after his commitment to his new way of life, Francis was beaten by robbers—and rejoiced about it.

~:~ He went to the Holy Land to preach to the Muslims, who greatly respected him.

~:~ Along with the Dominicans, Francis and his followers rebuilt the medieval Church by renewing it spiritually.

~:~ Within ten years, Francis' followers grew to more than five thousand.

~:~ Francis gave away the community's only prayer book, so they could give alms to a beggar.

~:~ Francis inspired his contemporary Saint Clare to begin the order that was eventually known as the Poor Clares.

~:~ Francis was the first known stigmatist—mystically, the wounds of Christ were reproduced physically on his body two years before his death.

~:~ Saint Francis didn't actually write the prayer, "Lord, make me an instrument of your peace."

~:~ When he wrote (and set to music) the exultant prayer, "The Canticle of the Sun," Francis was suffering excruciating pain.

~:~ He wanted to be buried in a cemetery for criminals.

~:~ "Friars Minor" is the name Francis gave to his new order (later known as Franciscans).

In His Own Words

"We adore you, O Lord Jesus Christ, here and in all your churches which are in the whole world, and we bless you, because by your holy Cross you have redeemed the world."

Reader's Guide for Saint Francis, page 169.

Saint Juan Diego

"Am I Not Your Mother?"

Born: 1474 in Tlayacac, Cuauhtitlán (north of present-day Mexico City)
Died: May 30, 1548
Feast Day: December 9
Canonized: July 30, 2002, by Pope Saint John Paul II
Patron: Mexico; those devoted to Our Lady of Guadalupe

On the cold morning of December 9, 1531, Juan Diego made his way along the dusty road to Tlatelolco (Tla-te-LOL-co), his usual route to attend Mass and to hear instruction from the priests. During the three-and-a-half-hour trip, he was thinking of how life had changed in these past ten years. The conquerors had come and taken away the greatness of his people. *Our land is now their land,* he thought. *They are our rulers; we are like slaves. However, I have accepted their religion because. . . .* Suddenly he heard the strains of lovely music. *What is it that I hear? Such music must be of heaven!* And then someone called his name, "Juanito," but with such sweetness, "Juan Dieguito."

He began to look around, staring off to the east, curious about the sounds he was hearing. He was so taken by the music that, without realizing it, he began climbing Tepeyac Hill. At the top he was surprised to find a beautiful young woman, not a Spaniard, but one of his own people, a morena. In an instant he took in the scene: she was standing in a field of emerald hues where the ground was usually brown and dusty; the blaze of sun was behind her, whereas it should have still been rising toward midday; her clothing was regal; and she appeared to be pregnant.

She was looking at him with such a loving expression, as if she really knew who he was. "Juanito," she continued. "My smallest child, where are you going?"

"My Mother," he replied, returning her gaze, "I am on my way to your house in Tlatelolco to hear the divine things taught by our priests, our Lord's delegates."

"Know and understand, dearest of my children," the lady continued, "that I am the ever-holy Virgin Mary, Mother of the true God who gives life, Mother of the Creator of heaven and earth. I have an ardent desire that a temple be built where I can show forth all my love, compassion, assistance, and defense because I am your loving Mother: yours, and all who are with you, and of all who live in this land, and of all who love me, call to me, and trust in me. I will hear their cries and will give remedy to their sorrows and sufferings."

As he listened, Juan Diego felt great love and confidence toward this motherly figure. She urged him, "So that I can actually show my mercy as I desire, go to the bishop and explain that I have sent you to manifest what I wish, that a temple be built for me on this very site." Without losing a moment, Juan Diego said, with a slight bow, "I am on my way to do as you ask, my Lady."

As he hurried along, Juan Diego reflected on what had happened. *My heavenly Mother did not suddenly appear to me as in a dream. No, she was right there speaking to me as a mother to her son. And I could address her as I would my own mother. I must hurry and faithfully carry out her wishes.* In his heart he kept hearing her voice calling, "Juanito, Juan Dieguito."

Although he was fifty-seven years old, Juan Diego had no difficulty covering the miles quickly. He was received at the door of the bishop's palace and directed to a place to sit until called. He sat quietly and waited, and waited, and waited, going over and over what he must say. Bishop Juan de Zumárraga was a kindly man, who when eventually informed of his visitor, invited him in. He listened attentively to Juan Diego but decided to give the story the test of time. "Thank you for what you have related to me, Juan Diego, but I must ask you to come again another day when there is more time. Then you can repeat what you have said and give me all the details." Juan Diego expressed his gratitude to the bishop, but outside he expressed his disappointment with a deep sigh.

Back at Tepeyac he again found his Lady waiting. "My dear Mother," he began, "I went and delivered your message, but I don't think the bishop believes me. He might think this is my invention. Please, give your commission to someone more worthy than I. I am nobody. I am like a tail or a dead leaf. You ask me to go where I do not belong. Forgive me for saying this. Do not be angry with me, my Lady."

Mary was looking attentively at Juan Diego when she replied, "My littlest one, my son, listen to me. There are many servants and messengers from whom I could choose, but I desire that you take my message so that through you my wish will be fulfilled. I beg and command you, my dearest son, go again tomorrow to the bishop. Greet him in my name and tell him that work must begin on my temple. Tell the bishop that I have personally sent you—I, the ever-holy Virgin Mary, Mother of God."

Again, this humble man accepted the Lady's mandate but feared he would be rebuffed a second time. After all, he was only a Native.

Early the next morning he made the trip once more to the bishop's residence, and once more he was made to wait. When kneeling before the bishop this time, Juan Diego was peppered with questions. Bishop Zumárraga wanted a description of the lady and the place where Juan Diego had seen her. Juan Diego held back nothing of what he had seen, of his impression of the lady, or of what she had requested of him. Even after all that, as he later recalled to his heavenly Mother, the bishop said he must ask for a sign, a proof of some kind that her appearance was true. In fact, however, the bishop was so intrigued that he sent men to follow Juan Diego, but they lost him somewhere near the hill.

He went home with the Virgin's assurance that tomorrow she would provide the sign the bishop requested. At home, to his dismay, Juan Diego found his beloved uncle, Juan Bernardino, very ill. He tried without success to find someone with medical expertise. So, early next day, Juan Diego set out for Tlatelolco to bring back a priest to anoint his uncle, now close to death. To avoid running into his Lady, Juan Diego went around the other side of Tepeyac Hill. In passing he glanced up at the hill just as Mary was descending toward him. "My little one, my son, what is happening? Where are you going?"

"My dear Lady," he stammered, "I hope you are well and happy, but what I tell you may sadden you. My uncle is dying, and I am rushing to call a priest to confess him and prepare him for death. As soon as I have done this, I will return to you. Please know I am being truthful. I will be back here tomorrow."

Looking at him with love, the Virgin assured him, "My son, fear not; what worries you now is nothing. Do not be frightened by that illness. Am I not your Mother? Your uncle will not die; believe me, he is healthy." Juan Diego was overjoyed by her words and immediately set off to do as she instructed. "Go, my son, to the top of the hill and collect the flowers you find. Bring them to me." At the place where he had first encountered the Lady, he found a large number of fresh, fragrant roses. When he presented all that he had cut to her, Mary took them from his arms and arranged them neatly in his cloak, or tilma. "Do not open your cloak for anyone but the bishop," she told him. "Tell him that I have sent you as my ambassador. You are most worthy of trust. Say that I sent you to the top of the hill to cut these flowers. Explain to him all that you saw and experienced so that he may be persuaded to build the temple I request."

This time, as Juan Diego knocked at the palace door, he felt sure of success, but again the servants tried to turn him away. As he pleaded for an audience with the bishop, one of the servants caught sight of what looked like a rose sticking out from under Juan Diego's tightly held garment. The man attempted to grab the flower, but Mary's ambassador held strong. Because of the tantalizing aroma of the roses, the servants finally decided to inform the bishop. He hurried from his study and invited his visitor to come in. Juan Diego gladly accompanied the bishop and after properly greeting him recounted his wondrous story from the beginning.

"Señor Bishop, as you ordered, I went to my Lady, Holy Mary, Queen of Heaven, and made your request. I told her that I had promised to bring a sign back for you. She agreed. And that is how, very early this morning, she sent me to the top of the hill, where I first met her, to cut roses. She herself arranged them in my tilma to be brought to you. Only cactus and dried brush grow on that hill, but this morning it was full of every variety of Castilian roses. Now I am to present them to you as her sign that I am to be trusted and that she truly wants her request to be granted."

As Juan Diego unfolded his tilma, not only did a glorious array of roses fall to the floor, but a stunning portrait of his Lady appeared on his tilma. Before the bishop and those present with him, the miraculous image of Mary, the Mother of God and of the Americas, our Lady of Guadalupe, was revealed on the poor, simple tilma of her faithful son.

Juan Diego was a man of his civilization, one that had been viciously subjugated, a member of a trusting people who had been sorely tried by their conquerors. Because of his personal openness to God's call, he epitomized the true disciple of Christ's kingdom, the poor in spirit. And he had personally met that kingdom's Queen. He had conversed with her. She had shown him the utmost love and respect and had commissioned him to begin the process of getting a temple built in her honor on the very place of their meeting. It was this very spot on which he now stood. "Most beloved and beautiful Lady, my Mother, my little one, I will be here always at your service. I will tell everyone about your tender concern for my people, for all people. I will lead them to you where they can lay down their burdens and lift up their hearts to you and to the Giver of Life."

He spent the rest of his life as caretaker of Our Lady's shrine and as spokesman for the Mother of God. This holy and humble man, ever faithful son that he was, can still inspire us when we visit the glorious Shrine of Our Lady of Guadalupe.

Personal Challenge

In the spirit of Saint Juan Diego, what is one way that God can use me, just as I am, to carry out his purposes?

Prayer

Saint Juan Diego, Cuautlatoatzin, "talking eagle," among your people the eagle is the messenger of the Divine. Truly you were the messenger of the Queen of Heaven, her most trusted son. Our Lady of Guadalupe met with you as one meets a friend, inviting you to cooperate with her in the great work of evangelization among your own people. Help us to be devoted to this Queen and to trust her with our needs and those of our world today. Inspire us with the openness of heart needed to hear and act upon God's word so that we too may be worthy of the Kingdom. Amen.

Facts About His Life

~::~ His given name, Cuautlatoatzin (Cuauh-tla-toA-tzin), means "speaking eagle" or "one who speaks like an eagle" in his native language, Nahuatl (Aztec).

~::~ He and his wife were early converts to the Catholic faith, though his wife died before the apparitions.

~::~ He worked as a farmer and a weaver of straw mats.

~::~ In studying the image on the tilma, scientists have found that a reflection of Juan Diego unfolding the tilma appears in the eye of Our Lady of Guadalupe. The bishop and several other people can also be seen.

~::~ For seventeen years, Juan Diego lived next to the shrine as caretaker and guide.

~:~ The *Nican Mopohua*, "here it is written," is the earliest extant document of the apparition.

~:~ The dialogue, in Nahuatl, refers to Juan Diego with suffix tzin, a sign of respect and tenderness ("Juantzin" or "Juan Diegotzin").

~:~ Juan Bernardino went to Bishop Zumárraga to explain his cure from smallpox.

~:~ In Nahuatl, the appearance of flower and song together designate the presence of the divine.

~:~ Tlatelolco, a suburb of Mexico City, means "in the little hill of land."

~:~ The *tilma* (cloak), which is still intact today, is made of maguey, or agave. Fabric made with maguey usually lasts just twenty years.

In His Own Words

"Please, give your commission to someone more worthy than me. I am nobody. I am like a tail or a dead leaf. You ask me to go where I do not belong. Forgive me for saying this. Do not be angry with me, my Lady."

Reader's Guide for Saint Juan Diego, page 172.

BLESSED ARE THOSE
WHO MOURN, FOR THEY
WILL BE COMFORTED.

Saint Germaine Cousin

God's Cinderella

BORN: 1579 in Pibrac, France (small village near Toulouse)
DIED: 1601 in Pibrac
FEAST DAY: June 15
CANONIZED: June 29, 1867, by Pope Pius IX
PATRON: those who suffer abuse and child abuse, people with illness and physical disabilities

In a cold, musty corner of the barn, Germaine peered through one of the cracks in the wall. The teenage girl had a clear view of the house. In the twilight, she could see the tall, familiar figure of her father trudging slowly toward the house.

Her stepmother, Madame Cousin, had been anxiously awaiting his return, and she didn't like to be kept waiting. When he got to the door he was greeted with, "Don't just stand there. Come in and close that door. You're late. What kept you?"

Back in the barn, Germaine winced as she heard that rasping voice. She watched the door shut, then she went over to the pile of straw where she slept. As she sank into the straw, one of the lambs wandered over to her.

"You're so soft and silent, little one," Germaine whispered as she caressed it. Taking care of the sheep had been her responsibility since she'd been very young. They were Germaine's constant companions and the closest thing she had to friends.

Meanwhile, inside the house, Laurent Cousin took off his hat. "Old man Larue needed me to finish up," he said.

"I've already heard that excuse four times this week." Madame Cousin shook her head and stirred the soup faster.

Happy to see their father, the children were already vying with one another, trying to be the first to greet him. After they had displayed all their exuberance in hugs and kisses, the family settled down to eat.

"Did anyone bring Germaine supper?" Laurent asked his wife.

"No. And no one will until after we have eaten. Come on now, before everything gets cold."

Laurent swallowed his soup. He didn't completely understand his wife's attitude toward Germaine. After the meal, he got up, took what leftovers he could, and went out to the barn. "Germaine! Germaine!" he called.

"Father!" Germaine ran as fast as she could. "How was your day, Father?"

"Fine! I brought your supper." Germaine and her father sat down together on a low pile of hay.

"Mother makes delicious bread," said the girl as she tore off a piece.

Laurent looked over his daughter—her crippled arm cradled on her lap, the ugly tumors growing on her neck. No wonder his second wife kept Germaine separate from her own children. Then Laurent saw the newly formed dark bruise on Germaine's good arm.

Germaine caught his gaze, put down her bread, and shifted her position so that he couldn't see the bruise anymore. She shrugged her shoulders as he looked at her. "Mother gets so impatient. Sometimes I think I am happier out here in the peace of the barn than she is." At her father's puzzled look, she explained. "In the quiet, I can sense God is with me. That makes me very happy."

Laurent studied his daughter's calm gaze, then his lips twisted in a wry smile. "Get a good night's rest."

Laurent got up and left the barn, her soft "Good night, Father," echoing in his ears. What could he do for his daughter? She was pleasant, obedient, and hardworking. But with her disfigurement and crippled arm, she would always be a burden. Germaine tried to help by her spinning, but she had no future. No one knew whether her condition was contagious, so she was not marriageable. Laurent knew that his wife felt the need to discipline Germaine, but Madame Cousin often took out her anger on Germaine in cruel ways. It's her or me, he thought wearily. Germaine had been an outcast for so long, she didn't seem to mind any more. Like her comment tonight—she sounded as if she pitied his wife! Laurent shook his head. He wouldn't speak to Madame Cousin about that.

At dawn, Germaine gathered the sheep to lead them out to pasture. But her stepmother stopped her. "Germaine, today I want you to take the sheep to pasture at the edge of the Bouconne Forest."

"Bouconne Forest?" Germaine exclaimed in surprise. "But what about the wolves?"

"You heard what I said. And if you let anything happen to those sheep, girl, you'd better not come home."

"Yes, Stepmother."

Germaine puzzled over her stepmother's latest whim. What was she trying to prove? The Bouconne Forest was known for the packs of hungry wolves that roamed there. Lately some people had reported seeing them venturing out of the forest in search of food. All the farm folk were so frightened that they avoided the area as much as possible.

Germaine did as her stepmother ordered. When it was good weather—and not too cold of a winter's day, like today—she enjoyed taking the sheep out. Alone with God's creatures, Germaine felt surrounded by God's love and majesty. As she did daily, she spent much of the day in prayer. Maybe she had no friends to talk to on earth, but talking to God was as real to her as breathing.

Today, she entrusted her safety—and that of the sheep—to God. The edge of the forest certainly provided plenty of good grazing. But the starving wolves prowled the area as well. Germaine could occasionally hear growls and the rustling of leaves, but she stayed calm.

Madame Cousin made sure she watched for Germaine to come home that night. Surprised to see her stepmother waiting for her, Germaine waved as she approached the barn, but Madame Cousin did not return the greeting. As soon as Germaine came up to her, she inspected the sheep and asked roughly, "Did you bring back all the sheep?"

"Yes, Stepmother," Germaine said.

"Are you sure? Did you count them? You're not lying to me, are you?" As she said this, Madame Cousin counted the sheep herself. "I guess you know what's good for you. Tomorrow you'll go back there again," Madame Cousin said coldly.

The following day, Germaine again pastured the sheep at the edge of the forest. As Germaine was busily spinning wool, she suddenly heard the rustling of leaves behind her. She turned quickly and saw a poor beggar coming up the forest path.

"Sorry if I startled you," the man called.

"You didn't startle me," stammered Germaine. "Would you care to join me?" She rummaged in her sack and pulled out a few crusts of bread. "You are welcome to what I have," she said as she offered them to him. Germaine seldom ate all the bread she was given. Each day she would make a little sacrifice and put some aside for anyone who needed food that day.

The man nodded his thanks as he reached for the crusts. "I was trying to get to the next village, and I started wondering if I was going to end up as food for the wolves. What are you doing, grazing your sheep here? Aren't you afraid that they will attack?"

"We are safe. God is watching over us," Germaine replied.

But the beggar was concerned for the kindly girl. "I'm telling you; they'll attack as soon as they feel sure of themselves."

"I have to go home now," Germaine said. "Maybe I'll see you tomorrow."

Germaine hurriedly gathered the sheep and headed home. When she had herded the sheep into their pen, she went to pull out the small supply of bread she had saved. She dug deep into the hay, but it was gone! All her scraps of bread, so carefully saved, had disappeared. While the girl had been at the forest that day, Madame Cousin had taken the few pieces of bread Germaine had put aside.

The girl's first thought was, "That poor man! What shall I give him if I see him tomorrow?"

Taking all her courage, Germaine headed to the forbidden house and went straight to the kitchen door. She tiptoed in and closed the door softly. Her eyes immediately fell on a basket. Picking up the cloth cover, she found the missing bread—even some straw still stuck to it. Germaine took the few stale pieces of bread, wrapped them in her apron, and stepped toward the door.

"What are you doing in this house, you dirty good-for-nothing?" Madame Cousin burst into the room. "Stealing my bread, are you? You won't get away with this!"

Enraged, Madame Cousin grabbed a large wooden stick and threatened to beat Germaine. The girl pulled her apron tightly to herself and ran. Her stepmother shouted after her, "Thief! Thief!"

The neighbors flocked out to see what was going on. They had never seen Madame Cousin so upset. She was screaming and running after Germaine with a stick! "If she catches up with her, she'll kill that poor girl," yelled one of the men.

Germaine's heart pounded as she gasped for air. With her poorly nourished body, she didn't have the strength to keep running. She stopped, defenseless, arms clutching her apron. One of the neighbors tried to hold Madame Cousin back from attacking Germaine. "Stop!" the woman gasped. "Don't hit her!"

Madame Cousin raised the stick and commanded, "Open your apron and show everyone what a thief you are!"

In front of everyone, Germaine dropped the hem of her apron. Instead of hard crusts of bread, out fell a beautiful assortment of spring flowers.

The neighbors started to murmur among themselves. "Where did she get those in the middle of winter?"

"It's a miracle, I tell you!"

Shocked, bewildered, and embarrassed, Madame Cousin felt her rage fade to confusion. She quietly told Germaine to go back to the barn.

Besides the miracle of the flowers, another miracle took place that day—a conversion in the heart of Madame Cousin. Although she never actually apologized to Germaine, she was no longer as harsh and cruel as she had been. Germaine was thrilled that her prayers for her stepmother had been answered.

But Germaine didn't enjoy the newfound peace in her life for long. One morning in the summer of 1601, Germaine was found dead on her bed of straw. To some people, her life of twenty-two years might seem to consist only of sickness, beatings, loneliness, and lack of love. Yet, within the tragedies of her life, the Church recognizes the glowing heroism of a simple, disfigured farmer's daughter who discovered, clung to, and witnessed to God's love in surprising ways.

On June 29, 1867, Pope Pius IX officially proclaimed her a saint.

Personal Challenge

In the spirit of Saint Germaine, who treated her parents with kindness and respect, regardless of the way they treated her, what is one act of charity I can do for someone who has hurt me?

Prayer

Saint Germaine, in the midst of life's tragedies—the loss of your mother and harsh abuse—you clung to the comfort and strength of

God's love for you. You didn't allow cruelty, loneliness, or suffering to embitter your heart but sought ways to alleviate the suffering of others. Unquenchable hope allowed you to discern God's love and providence in your life and in the world. When loss, suffering, and the unfairness of life threaten to overwhelm me, help me put that same trust in God, that he will comfort me in my suffering and give me the strength and compassion to stand up against injustice. Give me that transforming vision of faith to be open to how God can turn the most unlikely of events into an encounter of grace. Amen.

Facts About Her Life

~:~ Germaine had a great devotion to the Rosary, which she prayed daily using a knotted string.

~:~ Germaine left her sheep in the care of her guardian angel when she went to daily Mass. The sheep never wandered off and were never harmed.

~:~ Once, a villager saw the waters of the swollen river part for her, so she could get to Mass on time.

~:~ Visions and glorious music (witnessed by neighbors) sometimes accompanied Germaine's prayer.

~:~ Despite her poverty and sufferings, Germaine also fasted on bread and water.

~:~ In addition to a crippled hand, Germaine suffered from scrofula, a kind of tuberculosis of the neck.

~:~ In the sixteenth century, people with physical disabilities were often considered to be less than human. Germaine was considered a fool or an idiot by many in her village. Only gradually did the villagers recognize her holiness.

~:~ Many of the miracles attributed to Saint Germaine's intercession are connected to her own life: miraculous physical healings and the multiplication of food.

~:~ Germaine might have been forgotten if her body hadn't been accidentally discovered to be incorrupt in 1644, although it hadn't been embalmed.

~:~ During the French Revolution, her casket was desecrated by quicklime thrown on her body in an effort to destroy it. Afterward, her body was again found intact except where the quicklime had damaged it.

In Her Own Words

"Dear God, please don't let me be too hungry or too thirsty. Help me to please my mother. And help me to please you."

Reader's Guide for Saint Germaine, page 174.

Saint Monica

The Mother Who Never Gave Up

BORN: c. 331 in Tagaste, Numidia (now Algeria)
DIED: 387 in Ostia (in what is now Italy)
FEAST DAY: August 27
CANONIZED: By popular acclaim
PATRON: wives, wives who suffer abuse, mothers, widows

The dignified woman opened the door and stiffly walked into the room at the seaside inn. As she looked at the drab, empty room, she thought, *Nothing special about it.* It was simply supposed to be a stopover; it wasn't supposed to be the place where her heart would be broken . . . again.

She managed to hold in her tears until she closed the door behind her. Then, Monica collapsed on her knees beside the bed, burying her face in the cheap pillows and letting them absorb the sound of heartbreak.

First her husband, now her firstborn son. Monica felt so alone. How well she remembered the first time she'd wept like this—thirty years ago, on her wedding night. She had been young then and had expected a happy wedding night. After patiently putting up with the nagging interference of her mother-in-law all day, Monica had been stunned when her new husband, Patricius, flew into a rage. He had insulted Monica in front of all their guests and then went out into the night, abandoning her.

It had been a sad prelude to what much of her married life would be like—a hostile mother-in-law who delighted in stirring up her son's discontent, a husband's fearsome temper tantrums, abandonments, and infidelities. That night, vulnerable as only a bride can be on her wedding night, she had prayed fervently that her faith would sustain her.

"Dear God, please help me to be a faithful and good wife to Patricius. Help me to do your will and to show your love to him. If our wedding night means nothing to him . . . I'm terrified of the future. Help me! I mustn't think ahead. Help me now . . . just one day, one minute at a time." She had cried herself to sleep that night, and many nights thereafter, her tears alternating with her prayers, "Lord, just help me *today, now!*"

She had put up with her husband's fiery temper, dissolute habits, and infidelity for twenty years. She had found a "secret weapon"—the grace of Christian forbearance. Early on in her marriage, she had decided never to respond with anger when her husband or mother-in-law was angry. It had been impossible at first, and a constant effort—sometimes daily, sometimes minute--by-minute. But gradually, Monica found a way to keep her peace and be unwaveringly gentle, kind, and patient.

Despite her husband's infidelity and outbursts of anger, Patricius never struck her. Finally, after twenty years, Patricius asked to be instructed in the Christian faith. When he was baptized, he became another man. He lived a fervent Christian life for only a year before falling sick and dying. Monica's grief had been tempered by the joy of their last year together and the certainty that her husband had finally found the peace and happiness he had so longed for.

How she missed him now! Maybe he would have known what to do with their wayward son. Although Patricius had not agreed to have Augustine baptized, Monica had instructed her son in the beliefs and practices of Christianity. But as a teenager away at school, Augustine fell in with bad friends and rejected Christianity in favor of Manichaeism. Monica was brokenhearted when she learned of his rejection of faith. Manichaeism claimed to synthesize all religions through intellectual enlightenment and was particularly hostile to Christianity. Monica began to pray constantly for her son; she cried and begged God to lead Augustine to the truth. She talked and pleaded with him but with no results. His way of life was so immoral that, for a time, she had refused him entrance to the house. But then she quickly realized that shutting him out would neither change him nor help him.

One night, God comforted her with a vision. An angel appeared to her and addressed her gently, "Why are you crying? Dry your tears. Your son is with you." With that the angel pointed to Monica's right. There, in a vision, was her son—serene, calm, and resplendent in white. The next day she told Augustine, "Last night I saw a messenger from God. He told me that you were with me."

"Well, Mother," Augustine smirked, "are you coming over to our way of thinking?"

"No, son. I wasn't told that I was with *you*, but that *you* were with *me*."

Augustine couldn't hide the impression her quick answer made on him. But he didn't change. At times it seemed that the more she prayed for him, the deeper Augustine became enmeshed in immorality and error. She had begged one priest after another, one bishop after another, to speak to her son. To placate her, one bishop had told her, "It is impossible that a child of such tears and prayers will perish!" So Monica persevered in prayer. It was all she had to provide her with some sanity and hope.

And in these past few years, her son had softened toward her. While he still clung to his denial of Christianity, they spoke often. He had decided to go to Rome to teach rhetoric. Although he was only twenty-nine, he had been offered a prestigious position there. Concerned about his spiritual welfare, Monica had hoped to persuade him not to go. But he wouldn't yield, so she decided to go with him. Monica wanted to travel together. Augustine told her he had to visit friends and that they would leave the next day, so Monica spent the day in a nearby chapel. When she went to meet him in the morning, she discovered that he had deceived her again. "Their" ship had left the day before with Augustine on board. He had deliberately left her behind.

Now, kneeling by the bed, Monica dried her tears. What could she do? It was obvious Augustine wanted her nowhere near him. He had abandoned her. Should she simply go home? Pray for him from afar? She couldn't give up on him, no matter what.

Monica thought about her son: his stubbornness, his keen intellect, his self-honesty. She knew how sensitive Augustine would be as he continued to search for the truth. Although her words seemed to have no effect on him up till now, she didn't know what a difference her presence might make at the right moment. Could she really leave his spiritual welfare to strangers?

But it wouldn't be easy traveling without him. And how would she find him? Would he even stay in Rome? Monica sighed. She barely dared to ask herself her biggest question: What if when she found him, he fled her presence again?

Monica turned once again to the Source of her strength. What should she do? Should she risk being rejected again by her son? Should she stay behind or go to find him?

"Lord, you gave my beloved son Augustine into my care. Show me now how I can best help him to find you." In the throbbing quiet of sorrow, Monica received her answer. Just because he had abandoned her, she wouldn't abandon him. God *had* entrusted Augustine's well-being—body and soul—to her care. Perhaps, somehow, her mother's love would eventually help him to come to believe in God's love for him.

With renewed strength, Monica booked passage on the next ship to Rome. When she arrived, she found he had turned down the position and gone to Milan. So off she went to Milan.

After a long search, Monica finally found her son and learned from him that although he was not a Christian, he was no longer a Manichaean. Monica redoubled her prayers. Finally, with the wisdom and help of Saint Ambrose, the bishop of Milan, Augustine was baptized. He was thirty-two. Monica was overwhelmed with joy. With the friends who had been converted and baptized with him, Augustine went to a country villa where they could solidify their newfound faith with prayer, meditation, and discussions. Augustine wanted Monica to join them. Not only did she look after their needs, but she also contributed to their discussions.

Eventually Augustine and Monica decided to return home, and they traveled to the port city of Ostia, where they waited for a ship. One night Augustine and his mother were alone on the patio looking at the beautiful sky and God's magnificent creation and talking together about heaven. Eventually they both fell silent. For a brief moment, God gave them both an intuition of what the joys of heaven would be like. After sharing a profound silence, Monica spoke.

"Son, no longer do I find any joy in this life. I have received all I hoped for. My last desire—the one for which I lived—was to see you baptized and dedicated to God's service. Why I am still here on earth, I don't know."

A few days later Monica fell ill. She burned with fever for several days. In a lucid moment, she told Augustine, "You shall bury your mother here. It doesn't matter what happens to my mortal remains. Just promise to remember me every day at Mass, no matter where you are."

After only nine days of illness, Monica serenely passed away. Augustine was thirty-three years old. He suffered immense grief for his mother. But he did not cry at the funeral because she had died such a holy death. Later, however, when he was alone and thought about his mother's love, prayers, and constant care, he burst into tears and cried for the mother who had shed so many tears for him. He wrote, "If I am your child, O my God, it is because you gave me such a mother!"

Sixteen centuries separate us from Monica, yet she suffered the same tragedies that families face today: abuse, marital infidelity, the breakdown of the family, and family members who reject God and his commandments. She was an ordinary woman with no exceptional gifts, who was continuously disappointed by those whom she loved. Yet through these troubling, even tragic, circumstances of her life, she lived an extraordinary commitment to her vocation as wife and mother. Her perseverance in prayer, her fidelity to always being there for her husband and children, no matter how they responded to her, gradually worked the greatest miracle of all: the miracle of Love being born in their hearts.

Personal Challenge

When I am discouraged at the way my prayers for others seem to be unanswered, can I, like Saint Monica, persevere in faithful and trusting intercession for the salvation of those I love?

Prayer

Saint Monica, you were just an ordinary woman. No miracles, no extraordinary events filled your life. Instead, your cup was filled to overflowing with suffering and tears as your loved ones broke your heart many times over. Yet you never gave up on them, nor on God's love for them. Your extraordinary love of your husband and children wove the fraying threads of your family always more closely together. You trusted in the power of your motherly prayer to move God's heart, and your wayward son didn't just convert but became a great saint of the Church. In times of grief and suffering, when I mourn for my loved ones, give me that same confidence in God's love. May the ordinary sufferings of my life also become extraordinary through the power of God's love working in me and through me. Amen.

Facts About Her Life:

~:~ Monica was raised in a devout Catholic family.

~:~ As a youngster sent to draw the wine, Monica started to "taste" the wine and gradually started to drink cupfuls regularly.

When a servant caught her and called her a "wine-bibber," Monica stopped. Shortly afterward, she was baptized.

~::~ Monica's husband verbally abused her for almost twenty years.

~::~ In addition to her husband's conversion, Monica's patience also won over her ill-tempered mother-in-law.

~::~ Monica had two other children who survived to adulthood: Perpetua, who was married briefly and entered a monastery after she was widowed; and her younger son Navigius, who was also with her when she died. She also had four grand-children: Adeodatus, the son of Augustine and his mistress, and the three children of Navigius.

~::~ When Monica pleaded with priests and bishops to speak to her son, many of them dismissed her. Only Saint Ambrose, whom she met only a few years before she died, seemed to understand her.

~::~ Saint Ambrose became Monica's spiritual adviser, whom she promptly obeyed. When Saint Ambrose was being persecut-ed, Monica was one of those who stood vigil for him, risking her own safety. Saint Ambrose had a very high opinion of Monica and praised her to Augustine.

~::~ Monica had carefully prepared her own burial place next to her husband because she wanted even her physical remains to be united to his. But shortly before she died, Monica de-cided that it didn't matter where she was buried. She even lightheartedly joked that God would be able to find her re-mains wherever she was buried.

~::~ Monica's son Augustine became not only one of the most famous converts of the Church, but also one of the greatest saints of the early Church, receiving the title Father of the Church due to his many inspiring and profound writings about the faith and the tremendous influence they have had on the Church's life.

~:~ Almost everything we know about Saint Monica, we know from the writings of Augustine.

~:~ There is little record of devotion to Monica until the fifteenth century when her remains were discovered in Ostia and transferred to the church of Saint Augustine in Rome.

In Her Own Words

"Remember me at the altar of the Lord."

Reader's Guide for Saint Monica, page 176.

BLESSED ARE THE
MEEK, FOR THEY WILL
INHERIT THE EARTH.

Saint Bernadette

Unlikely Visionary

BORN: January 7, 1844, in Lourdes, France

DIED: April 16, 1879

FEAST DAY: April 16 in France. The universal Church fittingly celebrates the Feast of Our Lady of Lourdes on February 11, the anniversary of the first apparition.

CANONIZED: December 8, 1933, by Pope Pius XI

PATRON: France, those who are ill, those who are poor

A thick fog blanketed the little town of Lourdes, France, on this cold and damp morning. In the impoverished room that served as the Soubirous family home, Mama Louise was cleaning a few vegetables for the thin soup that would be the family's noon meal. The one-room former jail cell that served as their home had only three beds and a chair for furniture. The whole family shared the small quarters—Francois Soubirous; his wife, Louise; fourteen-year-old Bernadette; twelve-year-old Toinette; and their brothers, John and Justin. Mama Louise sighed as her daughters turned to leave for school.

"Bernadette," said her mother, "go straight to school and don't wander; your cough might come back."

"Don't worry, Mama, I'll put on my cloak and cap, so I won't be cold." Bernadette's eyes met her mother's, and she nodded an unspoken obedience.

On her way to school, Bernadette gulped the fresh air with relief. At home, the thick, stale air could make anyone choke, and Bernadette, whose asthma already made breathing difficult, often found it unbearable. At times she would stand by the barred window and gulp great draughts of the fresh, clean air that blew down from the Pyrenees Mountains. At night she could not do this without disturbing the family, so she would lie awake next to her sister Toinette, suffering as silently as possible, but letting a cough escape her now and then.

Today, she was happy to escape not only the choking air— she was also relieved to be free of her mother's too-penetrating gaze. She had told her parents last night how unhappy she was— she had to choose between obeying her parents or the Lady. She had promised her mother she would *try* to go straight to school, but she wanted *so much* to see the beautiful Lady again!

Bernadette had first seen the Lady only a few days ago, on February 11, 1858. Bernadette, Toinette, and their friend Jeanne Abadie were gathering firewood, as they often did. A short walk from home, the girls came to the River Gave at the grotto, or Cave of Massabielle. Toinette and Jeanne saw some sticks on the far side and waded across the river to get them, squealing as the icy water chilled their feet.

"Please throw some stones in so that I won't get my feet wet," Bernadette called. "Mama wouldn't want that!"

Jeanne, however, retorted, "You're such a nuisance! Stay where you are if you don't want to cross!" As the bells of Saint Peter's Church pealed out the Angelus and its echoes died away among the hills, Jeanne and Toinette quickly gathered the bits of wood near the river and moved farther off.

Bernadette was left alone. At first, she threw stones into the stream to make a path for her to cross, but the attempt failed, so she decided to take off her shoes and wade over as the others had done. Just then, she thought she heard a rumble of distant thunder—or was it a sudden gust of wind? Bernadette glanced about. She saw no storm clouds; nothing stirred. "I must have been mistaken," she thought, and bent down again to remove the shoe.

But then she heard that same sound! This time Bernadette stood up and looked about intently. What was happening? On the slope before her a wild rosebush was tossing violently as if caught in a gale. Everything else was still.

As Bernadette stared, the dark cave brightened, and a beautiful young Lady appeared over the rosebush. Bernadette felt numb. She rubbed her eyes, closed them, and reopened them, but the Lady was still there. Her warm smile told Bernadette that this was real, after all! Quickly she pulled her rosary from her pocket and began to pray. When she finished praying the Rosary, the Lady disappeared from view.

When the Lady was gone, Bernadette took her shoes off to wade through the stream, eager to join the other girls. To her surprise, the water wasn't cold, but lukewarm. Bernadette caught up to the others and asked if they had seen anything. They hadn't. Then they teased Bernadette, promising to tell no one, until she confessed that she had seen "a lady in white."

That afternoon, Toinettte let the news of the Lady slip out. Bernadette's mother was unusually serious. "You must get these ideas out of your head, Bernadette," she decided. "I'm not sure you should go to Massabielle again!" The joy of Bernadette's meeting with the Lady was immediately mixed with the pain of her parents' disapproval. But the Lady had asked her to come back fifteen more times, and Bernadette had promised to return. With the reluctant permission of her parents, who were influenced by curious relatives and friends, Bernadette had already gone back to the grotto several times.

Daily, Bernadette alternately faced ridicule, scorn, threats, demands of proof, and adulation. While Lourdes buzzed with rumors and ridicule, she tried to go about her usual daily duties. Poorly educated, unable to even read and write, the humble girl hardly seemed likely to be favored by heaven.

Then one night, Police Commissioner Jacomet waylaid her, interrogated her, and threatened her father with jail. Her parents, worried about the commissioner's threats, forbade Bernadette to go back to the grotto.

Bernadette managed to make it to school and back home for lunch. But she could focus only on the Lady at the grotto. What would the Lady think if Bernadette broke her promise?

As Bernadette went back to school that afternoon, she could no longer resist the suddenly irresistible pull. She found herself heading toward the grotto!

Two policemen and a crowd of about one hundred people followed Bernadette. She arrived at the grotto and knelt in her usual place . . . but the Lady did not come that day. Shaken with shame, Bernadette was inconsolable. Her Aunt Bernarde pulled

Bernadette away. All the girl could say was, "I don't know how I've failed the Lady."

That evening, Bernadette went to her confessor and explained the situation. He thought that she should be allowed to go to the grotto. When Bernadette talked it over with her parents, they realized how distressed their daughter had become, and Francois Soubirous immediately relented.

Bernadette suffered from a storm of opposition: the town officials questioned her; neighbors ridiculed her; and the clergy tested her in various ways. Despite it all, Bernadette returned to the Lady for a total of eighteen apparitions. Her faithful obedience to the Lady was tested most dramatically when, during one apparition, the Lady told her to drink from and wash in the spring. Bernadette started to go toward the river, but the Lady called her back and indicated another area. Bernadette saw no spring or water, only mud. When the Lady repeated herself, Bernadette went over to the muddy spot, dug, and finally succeeded in finding a palmful of dirty water. Obedient to the Lady, she drank it—although she had a hard time swallowing it. Then, she "washed her face" in the muddy water, streaking it with dirt. As she left the grotto, her aunt tried to wipe her face clean, but the crowd undoubtedly thought she was crazy.

But that afternoon, the trickle of water Bernadette had dug up grew into a stream of clear water. Within a month, at least two people who washed in the spring water were inexplicably cured. The miraculous spring still flows today, and healings that cannot be explained by medical science continue to occur.

At one of the last apparitions, the Lady of the grotto finally revealed her name: "I am the Immaculate Conception." Bernadette, who was still preparing to receive her First Communion, didn't know what that meant. She repeated the mysterious phrase all the way to the pastor's house so that she wouldn't forget the Lady's name. After telling the pastor later in the day, she had the courage to ask the meaning of the words. She was overjoyed to learn that "the Immaculate Conception" was indeed Mary, the Mother of God.

The Virgin's message to Bernadette, and through her to the world, was simple and timeless: "Pray and do penance for sinners." For the rest of her short life, Bernadette strove to live this mandate of the Lady and to testify to what she had seen and heard. Although the constant questions exhausted her, she would remind herself that the Lady hadn't promised happiness in this world, but "in the other."

Not long after the final apparition, Bernadette went to live at the local convent of the Sisters of Charity and worked as their maid. Nothing contented her more than remaining small and hidden. Eventually she decided to ask to enter their community. The day she left Lourdes to enter the postulancy at Nevers was very difficult. She was leaving not only her family, but also the place where she had seen the beautiful Lady.

As a postulant at Nevers, Bernadette was assigned to washing pots and pans in the kitchen. Her superiors, desiring to keep her humble, would often humiliate her in front of others. Even on the joyful day of her profession of vows, when the bishop gave the newly professed sisters their assignments, Bernadette didn't immediately receive an assignment because the superior told him publicly, "She is good for nothing." Bernadette didn't object, but the situation must have been very painful for her. The truth was that her health was frail, and she needed the protection of the motherhouse from the prying public. At the same time that the superiors humiliated her, they recognized her virtue: novices who were going through difficulties were sent to talk to Bernadette because her kindness and directness encouraged them and resolved their difficulties.

Eventually, Bernadette was assigned to help in the infirmary; two years later she was given the position of sacristan, a duty she loved because it obliged her to spend many hours in the chapel. But her health, which had always been poor, was now failing rapidly. Soon she returned to the infirmary but as a patient. In her months of spiritual and physical suffering—both excruciating—Bernadette remained strong in character and never swerved from the course the Immaculate Virgin had shown her: to pray and to do penance for sinners. One of Bernadette's dearest hopes had been to return to Lourdes, to visit once more the grotto so dear to her. Her superiors even hoped that she might be healed there. But poor health and other obstacles prevented her from ever returning.

As she was dying, Bernadette was accompanied by her sisters. Her last prayer was to the beautiful Lady she so longed to see again, "Holy Mary, Mother of God, pray for me, a poor sinner."

Personal Challenge

In the spirit of Saint Bernadette, pray about one situation in your life where you can become more trusting in the power of God at work in you and others.

Prayer

Saint Bernadette, God favored you with the special grace to see his Mother many times while you were on earth. Instead of allowing this to go to your head, you let the attention—both friendly and hostile— root you more firmly in the truth that you were chosen so that others could know of God's great love and mercy. Always aware of your littleness, you put yourself fully at the service of the message entrusted to you. Help us to draw closer to the ever-beautiful Virgin Mary, Mother of God, so that she can lead us to Christ, and we can more fully experience God's mercy and share it with those who need it most. Amen.

Facts About Her Life

~::~ Bernadette was "small" not only in her humility but also physically, being only four feet seven inches tall.

~::~ Bernadette was the saint's nickname; Bernadette's baptismal name was Marie Bernarde, which she also received as her profession name.

~::~ Bernadette contracted cholera when she was six years old, and after that her health was never good. She suffered from both asthma and stomach ailments.

~::~ The Virgin Mary appeared to Bernadette eighteen times in all. Her message was a twofold invitation: Do penance for the conversion of sinners and come to pray at the grotto.

~::~ The hidden, muddy spring that Bernadette dug up at the request of the Blessed Mother produces thousands of gallons of water each week and has been attributed as the source of many miraculous cures inexplicable to modern medicine.

~:~ Bernadette's attraction to service—especially nursing the sick—helped her to discern her call to the Sisters of Charity.

~:~ The Lady used the respectful form of you—*vous*—when addressing Bernadette, and spoke to her in her dialect, not in standard French. This allowed Bernadette to understand the Lady but made her account of the apparitions less credible to the better-educated.

~:~ Bernadette is the first canonized saint to be photographed while she was alive.

~:~ Bernadette worked hard to tame her spontaneous reactions; occasionally she talked about her "boiling nature."

~:~ When Bernadette entered as a postulant at Nevers, she was invited to speak once to all the sisters about the apparitions. After that, none of the sisters in the community was ever allowed to speak to her about them again.

~:~ Her superiors often called on Bernadette to talk about the apparitions to bishops and other special visitors.

In Her Own Words

"My Jesus, fill my heart with so much love that one day it will break just to be with you."

Reader's Guide for Saint Bernadette, page 178.

Saint Gregory the Great

Servant of the Servants of God

BORN: c. 540 in Rome

DIED: March 12, 604, in Rome

FEAST DAY: September 3 (anniversary of his consecration as Pope in 590)

CANONIZED: By popular acclaim immediately after his death

PATRON: England, musicians, singers, teachers, victims of plague

The year was 590. For almost two centuries, Europe had been overrun by barbarian invasions, which brought terror, killing, and devastation everywhere. Rome itself had been sacked repeatedly. In only twenty years, it had been conquered four times. Now, flooding and famine had set off a plague that was devastating the population of Rome. News arrived at Saint Andrew's monastery that the plague had just taken the life of their pope, Pelagius II.

The frail but erect abbot pondered the latest tragedy and made it the subject of his prayer. "Lord, whom will you choose to guide your people now? Whoever it is, give him the grace, light, and strength to bear this heavy burden." The people would need the consolation of their clergy, and since the abbot also served as deacon of Rome, he must go immediately. He rose from his prayer as one of the monks came running in.

"Gregory, they are calling for you—" the breathless monk gasped out.

"I am on my way," Gregory nodded.

"—to be the new pope!" the monk managed to get out.

Gregory's spare frame froze as his mind started to race. This couldn't be! God had given him a monastic vocation, in which he was deeply happy. "Don't worry; they'll change their minds," Gregory told his brother monk. "God is not calling *me* to be pope! But our people need comfort, and we need to see what else can be done to stop the plague."

Gregory immediately set about helping the city out of its current crisis. From the pulpit, he announced that the people would hold a great procession through the streets of Rome, offering public prayer and penance for the end of the plague. The procession lasted for three days, with the people chanting, "Lord, have mercy." But even as they walked through the streets, both watchers and marchers fell ill and died. Still, Gregory walked with them, and after the procession of faith was completed, the plague quickly disappeared.

The clergy, officials, and people of the city adamantly declared Gregory the new pope. Despite all their arguments, he remained unconvinced. His appointment had to be approved by the emperor (see third point in Facts About His Life on page 60), and Gregory saw an easy way to resolve the situation. Along with the request for confirmation, he sent a personal letter asking the emperor not to confirm his appointment. But unknown to Gregory, the prefect of the city replaced Gregory's letter with one of his own, begging the emperor to confirm Gregory's appointment.

During the months Gregory waited for word from the emperor, he continued to serve his beloved Church and the city. But daily, he interiorly argued with himself. He cherished his monastic vocation, more so now because it had been tested several times—even by the previous pope. Gregory mused, "God has truly led me throughout my life; he will make his will clear."

Gregory was born of wealthy Roman nobility with deeply Christian roots. Two of Gregory's aunts (his father's sisters) were considered saints. Gregory's own mother, Sylvia, would also be acknowledged a saint. Gregory was as well educated as he could be in a city that suffered constant chaos from invasion and oppression. His studies in law enabled him to follow his father into civil service. Energetic and wise, with a keen sense of the law, he was a popular and successful politician. At the age of thirty, he took the highest civil office in the city—prefect of Rome.

Yet, after only a short time, Gregory felt God was calling him to a different kind of service. He gave up his position and much of his estate, using some of it to establish seven Benedictine monasteries, including one at his own home, where he himself became a monk.

Those had been the happiest years of his life. He dedicated himself completely to prayer, penance, and pastoral ministry. Yet, his happy seclusion was short-lived. Despite his reluctance to leave the monastery, Gregory obediently accepted when the Pope appointed him one of the seven deacons of Rome, thrusting him into a more active role in the Church. When Rome was once again besieged—this time by the Lombards—the Pope sent a delegation to Constantinople to beg for military assistance, appointing Gregory as papal ambassador.

The magnificent center of the Eastern Mediterranean world, Constantinople was a far cry from the pillaged ruins of Rome. Yet once there, Gregory did not see how he could succeed in his mission. He was at a disadvantage because he didn't speak Greek, and he refused to take part in the many court intrigues. He was troubled by signs of corruption in the government and evidence of heresy in the clergy, with whom Gregory heatedly debated. The emperor was too occupied fighting his own battles against the Persians to offer help to Rome. The failure of the mission became conclusive proof, in Gregory's mind, that God had called him to life in the monastery. After six long years, Gregory had happily returned to monastic life, serving as abbot in addition to his responsibilities as deacon.

Now, as Gregory used the time of waiting to examine the trajectory of his life, it seemed clear that God was calling him to continue as a simple monk. "Perhaps," he mused to himself, "one day I will be able to fulfill my dream to become a missionary to England."

After six months, word arrived from Emperor Maurice. Gregory's appointment had been confirmed, much to his consternation! Dismayed, Gregory immediately thought about fleeing the city. Instead, he fled to the monastery chapel.

There, Gregory wrestled with himself. How could *he* become pope? He overwhelmingly desired to offer his life for the world through prayer and suffering—the life of a simple monk. Gregory didn't feel himself worthy. He wasn't even a priest—just a deacon. He had no desire to become immersed in the affairs of Rome! In the absence of any real political authority, Gregory knew that whoever served as the next pope would also need to act as protector of the people.

Yet, despite his own desires, Gregory's path was no longer clear to him. How could he in good faith ignore the pleas of the people, the officials, and even the emperor when they were all raised together? Could God be speaking to him through the needs of the people? After a great deal of prayer, it seemed after all that despite his immense reluctance, it was God's will that he *should* become pope.

On September 3, 590, after being ordained a priest, the new pope and bishop of Rome was consecrated as Pope Gregory I. In his writings, he speaks often of this sacrifice: "My poor soul is forced to endure the burden of secular business . . . and returns back far less fit to think upon those affairs that are inward, spiritual, and heavenly . . . When I remember my former state of life, I cannot but sigh to look back upon the forsaken shore."

Yet Gregory's struggle to continue his intense prayer life amid his astounding achievements is not evident when we look at the lifetime of service he crammed into his short thirteen years as pope. Gregory brought a wealth of managerial genius and pastoral energy to the papacy. At heart a true pastor, his first concern was the welfare of the people. He gave down-to-earth sermons, aimed at nurturing the spiritual lives of his flock. These centered on Gospel themes—his favorite topics—and each sermon ended with a practical, moral conclusion. Gregory's writings are recognized more for their excellent summaries of the theological works of other Fathers of the Church than for being original. Gregory also reformed the liturgy and established guidelines for promoting the use of sacred music in the liturgy, especially encouraging and even teaching chant (which received his name in honor of his support). He also paid special attention to the formation of the clergy. His *Book of Pastoral Care* was used as a guide for bishops and priests throughout the Middle Ages.

Pope Gregory's care for the people was not confined exclusively to the pulpit and the spiritual life of his flock, although these always took precedence. Gregory urged social reforms for the poor and underprivileged, including land reforms for the more humane treatment of servants and tenant farmers. His huge charities—which took every form of relief imaginable—saved multitudes from starving and also ransomed countless prisoners from the invaders overrunning southern Europe. He strongly urged bishops to do the same, recommending they even sell church property when needed to raise the ransom for prisoners of war. He also sought to protect the rights of the Jewish people against unjust treatment and oppression, convincing one town to restore a synagogue to its Jewish citizens.

When, in 593, a barbarian army approached the walls of the city, Pope Gregory himself went out to meet the invading army and negotiated a truce that spared Rome and the surrounding areas another ruthless round of sacking and killing.

As Pope, Gregory was able to achieve one of his greatest desires: that of spreading the Gospel to England. While still a monk, Gregory had been saddened to learn that the Gospel had not yet been preached in England. Eager to give everyone the opportunity to learn about Christ, he resolved to go to Britain himself as a missionary. However, when wind of Gregory's plan reached the ears of his superiors, he was forced to abandon it and continue what he had already begun nearer home.

Now Gregory shared this deep desire with Saint Augustine of Canterbury, whom he sent to lead a band of monks to begin evangelizing in England. The Pope followed the missionaries' efforts closely and encouraged them in the dangers they faced.

His secretary, the deacon Peter, testified that Gregory never took a rest or vacation, even though he suffered from various chronic ailments. The severity of his monastic penances compromised his health, leading to stomach problems that tormented him for the rest of his life. Ill health prevented him even from rising on some days, but he continued to work from bed. In the end, Gregory's physical frame was reduced to almost a skeleton. Yet he continued to dictate letters and to look after Church affairs. After Pope Leo the Great, Gregory was only the second pope to have the title "the Great" added to his name. Yet, in his humility, while he decisively defended the authority of the papacy, he never personally became attached to the authority of his office. Instead, he called himself the "servant of the servants of God"—a title still used by his successors.

Gregory's last action on earth was to send a warm winter cloak to a poor bishop who suffered from the cold. This final act of charity characterized Gregory's entire life of loving and generous service.

Personal Challenge

Like Saint Gregory, who had to take up a ministry that he didn't actually want nor feel prepared for, can I see the hand of God at work in the opportunities that come my way in life?

Prayer

Pope Saint Gregory, how you lived the paradox of the Gospel! While Christlike in meekness, you fearlessly shepherded the Church and defended its rights. You unified a profound life of prayer with your availability to serve the needs of the world. You discovered God's invitations not just through his word but in the signs of the times and the needs of the Church. Enlighten me to understand the call of the Gospel: to be "in the world but not of it," and to be faithful to a vital life of prayer. Help me to allow God's love for me to shape my life and my response to others' needs. By your example, teach me the humility of service and the courage of true leadership. Protect the Church today, also living in perilous times, and ask for us the gift of your spirit of generous service. Amen.

Facts About His Life

~:~ Gregory made several significant career changes through his life: from politician to monk to pope.

~:~ When Gregory was called out of the monastery to serve the Church, he brought a few brother monks with him wherever he went.

~:~ In the sixth century, popes were elected by the clergy, the senate, and the people of Rome, and the Byzantine emperor confirmed the appointment. That's why Gregory almost refused the office of pope twice.

~:~ Gregory was the first monk to become pope.

~:~ In the chaotic breakdown of civil and military power, Gregory was such an effective administrator that, as pope, he was virtually the civil leader of Rome as well as the leader of the universal Church.

~::~ Gregory liked to tell stories in his homilies.

~::~ Gregory was criticized for emptying the Church's treasury to help the poor.

~::~ Gregory suffered severely not only from constant indigestion but also from gout.

~::~ In many ways, Pope Gregory I could be considered the architect of the Church in the Middle Ages—and thus of the Church today. His influence is still felt in many areas of Church life. Gregory may have written some of the prayers still used at Mass today.

~::~ After Pope Leo the Great, Gregory was only the second pope to be given the title "the Great."

~::~ By calling himself "the servant of the servants of God," Gregory was simultaneously expressing humility, reaffirming the universal authority of the papacy, and rebuking an Eastern patriarch for using a title that claimed Petrine authority (arising from Saint Peter, the first pope).

In His Own Words

"For one who undertakes the office of preaching ought not to do but rather to suffer wrong, and so by his meekness calm the anger of his persecutors, and heal the wounds of sinners, though weighed down himself by affliction."

Reader's Guide for Saint Gregory, page 180.

BLESSED ARE THOSE
WHO HUNGER AND THIRST
FOR RIGHTEOUSNESS,
FOR THEY WILL BE FILLED.

Saint Pier Giorgio Frassati

A Hunger for Holiness

Born: April 6, 1901, in Turin, Italy
Died: July 4, 1925, in Turin, of acute poliomyelitis
Feast Day: July 4
Canonized: September 7, 2025, by Pope Leo XIV
Patron: World Youth Day, athletes, young people

"Mama," the young man called as he rushed up the stairs, "tell Papa I'm out this weekend. Off to the mountain with the crowd." As he galloped back down loaded with his climbing gear, Pier Giorgio almost ran into his father.

"Whoa, whoa, son! What is the rush here, Giorgetto?" cajoled Signor Frassati. "Supper is almost on the table. Surely you will stay home with us tonight."

"No, Papa. Sorry. Must go, must go!" Blowing a kiss to his mother, out he went into the night.

"I don't understand that boy, Adelaide," Signor Frassati said to his wife. "I had hoped he would follow me into journalism. So much in our society needs straightening out, but no, he is supposedly studying engineering. Supposedly, I say, because he never seems to be in school."

"Oh, Papa," interjected Pier Giorgio's sister Luciana. "Of course you are upset, but we all know Giorgio is the apple of your eye."

"Yes, I admit it. He is a wonderful son. Just exasperating sometimes. He seems determined to give away everything he owns. And everything we own if we let him. Did you note the sack of 'gear' he had with him? His life is all friends and fun. It is time he settled down."

It was true. Pier Giorgio Frassati was often involved in adventures. Sometimes he seemed to be more interested in having a good time than in being responsible. However, Pier Giorgio was a good-natured, upright young man with a definite goal in mind. He was a man who lived the Beatitudes, intent on being a genuine disciple of Christ. In fact, his intention in choosing to pursue a degree in engineering was to be able to live and work among miners, to assist them in their social needs, but especially to help them to fully live out their Christian vocation.

As a child Pier Giorgio had already understood the living connection between Christ and his followers. He was only four years old when he spontaneously gave his shoes and stockings to the child of a beggar. At seven he ran to his mother pleading that she intercede with his father who had just closed the door on a poor man. "Mama," he cried, "what if Jesus sent that man to us?" This concern grew and deepened within Pier Giorgio as he matured. As a young man he spent a good deal of time secretly visiting and serving the poor of Turin. Countless stories tell of how he would spend his last coins on food, clothing, medicine, or fuel for the poor. One classic account concerns his graduation gift. His father, Alfredo, offered his Giorgetto the choice of a car or the equivalent in money. Pier Giorgio, of course, opted for the money. His father assumed his fun-loving boy planned to spend it entertaining his many friends. Little did he know that his son used it to entertain the needs of his very special friends, the poor and needy.

Pier Giorgio did indeed intend to settle down. He had fallen in love with Laura Hidalgo, a friend from his student group and a member of his mountain climbing club. He told no one of his infatuation with Laura; in fact, he had never even broached the subject with her. He recognized in her a soul companion, someone virtuous, hardworking, and compassionate, with whom he could build a solid Christian marriage. He feared, however, that his parents would not approve. They had other expectations for him, imagining that because his father had been a senator and an ambassador to Germany he would marry into the higher social class. Hoping for a sign of their acceptance, he hatched a secret plan to introduce the girl of his dreams to his family. On the chosen day she and two other young women were his guests for tea. Mother and Luciana had an opportunity to meet his love without anyone knowing his plan. The encounter was very revealing, but not as Pier Giorgio had hoped. Neither his mother nor his sister was favorably impressed. Judicious comments were made about his lovely friends who were obviously in over their heads at the former ambassador's residence. Pier Giorgio was heartbroken and remained silent about his hope. He confided later to a friend: "How deeply saddened I am. I was so ready to reveal my intentions to Laura, but now I must hold them inside. God must want me to concentrate more on my spiritual life." He could not be chided into going against his parents' wishes that he make "a good match." His parents lived in a state of constant tension and bickering, and, as Pier Giorgio later said, he could not bring himself "to break one family in order to begin another." His own heart would have "to pay the price."

Pier Giorgio seemed to be a contradiction of qualities. He wasn't rowdy, but exuberant with the pure-hearted joy of youth, a well-known practical joker, an instigator of fun and ferment. He was always a leader, but in an unassuming way. He never shied away from confrontation in order to defend principles. Once when Pier Giorgio was defending the rights of the Christian students' group, the police roughed him up. When they realized that he was the son of Senator Frassati, Pier Giorgio refused any special treatment. He remained with the students and waved their torn and dirty banner as a badge of honor. Another time Fascist ruffians burst into his parents' house. These troublemakers began to break up furniture and smash windows until Pier Giorgio grabbed a fireplace poker and chased them all out into the street. Satisfied that they were gone for good, he calmly returned to table and resumed eating his dinner.

From his youngest years Pier Giorgio enjoyed the challenge of sports, especially hiking, mountain climbing, and skiing. Sometimes he enjoyed going out alone to contemplate the beauties of God's creation, and at other times he enjoyed the company of friends. On these excursions, he was the life of the party. He would sing at the top of his notoriously off-key voice. If his friends objected, he would say, "I don't care one bit. The important thing is the singing!" For Pier Giorgio times of fun always included some moments for prayer. On these trips he would disappear into wayside shrines for prayer. The Rosary was so much a part of his daily routine that calling out the "Aves" on a trek up a mountain was as natural to him as breathing in the crisp air. His companions, motivated by his example, would enthusiastically answer. He unassumingly prayed the Rosary as he walked the streets of Turin and as he visited the sick to console and to aid them.

To support his many good intentions and charitable works Pier Giorgio joined many organizations, including the Saint Vincent de Paul Society, the Catholic Student Federation, Catholic Action, Milites Mariae, Apostleship of Prayer, the Company of the Most Blessed Sacrament, and the Cesare Balbo Club at the Royal Polytechnic University of Turin. He was everywhere and anywhere that needed a voice for justice. And he spent much time in adoration of the Blessed Sacrament.

In June 1925 his grandmother began her journey toward death. Around that time, Pier Giorgio began to feel a great deal of pain, which quickly sapped his energy and left him with an advancing paralysis. It seems that during one of his pilgrimages to the poor he had contracted the dreaded poliomyelitis virus. He was never one to oversleep, but now he found he needed more rest. In the frenzy of caring for her own dying mother, his mother lost patience with Pier Giorgio, thinking he was being inconsiderate. She scolded him, "Son, you are being so thoughtless. Grandmother is dying, and you are carrying on over a little flu."

In just five or six days the health of this robust young man had deteriorated to the point that he could not get up from bed. Doctors offered little hope to the Frassati family. They made a frantic effort to obtain a useful serum from Paris, but a thunderstorm delayed the plane. Pier Giorgio knew the Lord awaited him. True to his nature, he focused his last thoughts on others:

Would his parents be all right without him? Would others continue his visits to the poor? Would Luciana help him write a note about the medicine needed for one man and a policy to be renewed for another? These things weighed on his generous heart more than the thought of his own death.

"The day of my death will be the best day of my life," he had said a year earlier. That day, July 4, certainly brought untold blessings to Pier Giorgio's family and friends. At the funeral his family became acutely aware of the depth of their loss. While they were comforted by the presence of all the influential people of Turin who had gathered within the church for the funeral, it seemed that the rest of the city was outside. Hundreds of Turin's poor and troubled citizens paid their respects to the Frassatis' son. They were brothers and sisters whom Pier Giorgio had cared for in such a Christlike manner. Now his family understood his apparent inability to hold on to money, his habitual lateness, his nocturnal wanderings, his coy replies to their questioning. Pier Giorgio had ascended the Lord's mountain not merely by his athletic climbs but by his hidden and heroic charity.

Personal Challenge

In the spirit of Saint Pier Giorgio, who went about growing in holiness in ordinary ways, what is one act of kindness I can do for someone who is in need?

Prayer

Saint Pier Giorgio, you answered the psalmist's cry, "Who can climb the mountain of the Lord?" (see Ps 24:3) You climbed the mountain of holiness by your many steps to the homes of the poor; you held fast with your tenacious love for life; you breathed in the pure, crisp air of prayer and exhaled from your whole being the spirit of the living God. Teach us your secret hunger and thirst to live Gospel holiness within the parameters of our own lives. Help us concentrate on what truly matters. Amen.

Facts About His Life

~:~ His full name is Pier Giorgio Michelangelo Frassati, and he had the nicknames Dodo (as a child) and Terror (as a young man).

~:~ In junior high, he failed the Latin examination twice.

~:~ He liked to smoke a pipe.

~:~ He signed his many letters with *"Saluti in* G.C." (Greetings in Jesus Christ).

~:~ In 1918, he joined the Confraternity of the Rosary, the Saint Vincent de Paul Society, and the Italian Alpine Club.

~:~ He also began studies toward mining and an engineering degree. (He was preparing for exams when he died.)

~:~ In 1920, he joined the Peoples' Party and the Nocturnal Adoration Society.

~:~ His father, Alfredo, was appointed ambassador to Germany in 1921. Pier Giorgio stayed in Freiburg with the family of the Jesuit theologian Karl Rahner.

~:~ Pier Giorgio joined the Dominican Third Order in 1922, taking the name Girolamo (Jerome) in honor of the Renaissance Florentine cleric Savonarola. He also joined the Legion of Mary.

~:~ In 1923, he helped to found the Shady Character Society, calling himself "Citizen Robespierre."

~:~ When exhumed in 1981, Pier Giorgio's body was found to be incorrupt.

~:~ His tomb is at a side altar in the Cathedral of Turin.

~:~ The miracle for his canonization was the instantaneous healing of Los Angeles seminarian Juan Gutiérrez, who tore his Achilles tendon when playing basketball.

~:~ Pope Saint John Paul II called him "the man of the eight Beatitudes."

In His Own Words

"It is to Jesus that I go. He comes to me each morning in Holy Communion. I repay him in a small way by visiting the poor."

Reader's Guide for Saint Pier Giorgio, page 182.

Venerable
Teresita Quevedo

The Champion

BORN: in Madrid on April 14, 1930
DIED: April 8, 1950, in Madrid of tubercular meningitis
DECLARED VENERABLE: June 9, 1983, by Pope Saint John Paul II
PATRON: students, young athletes, novices, devotees of Mary

Dashing across the tennis court, sixteen-year-old Teresita Quevedo bumped into a girl she knew.

"Hi, Teresita," her friend called. "I hear you're in the tennis competition today. Did you warn them you'll need an extra-large crown if you win; your head is way too big for the normal size."

Teresita laughed as she sped off to begin her set.

When she returned home that evening, Teresita greeted her mother with a big smile.

"Well, Teresita," Señora Quevedo asked. "Do we have a champion in the family?"

The girl paused, and her eyes filled with tears.

"No, Mama," she replied. "Not really, at least not the way you have in mind. But if you consider the winner of a spiritual victory a champion, then you have one."

Señora Quevedo was aware of her daughter's desire to win a tennis championship before graduating from high school. She knew Teresita had prepared nonstop and that she was clearly everyone's favorite. So she gently encouraged, "Tere, tell me what happened."

"Mama," Teresita began, "I told the Blessed Mother that I was leaving it in her hands. I'm afraid I wanted the win more out of vanity than anything else. And so I stopped at church on the way home to tell her I was happy she decided that my opponent should win instead of me. I saw an old lady begging at the church door, and I gave her an offering. When she thanked me, she gave me a holy card. It wasn't a picture but only an inscription in large blue print. Can you guess what it said, Mama?"

"No, Teresita, tell me," her mother said.

With a victor's smile Teresita replied, "*Love makes all things easy.*"

A few months later, trusting in these words, Teresita slipped into her father's room.

"Papa," she whispered, "are you asleep?"

"No, come in, Teresita," Doctor Quevedo invited. "What can I do for you?"

Teresita walked close to him and began, "Papa, I dread telling you this because it's going to hurt you, but . . ."

"Go on, tell me, Teresita. What is it you want?"

"I want to become a Carmelite, Papa."

"Teresita, do you realize what that means? You are so full of life—so fond of sports . . . dancing . . . and parties . . ." His voice trailed off.

"Yes, but none of that satisfies me, Papa."

"My dear child, do you know that religious lead a life of sacrifice?"

"Yes, Papa, I know. That's why I want to enter the convent."

"And," her father continued, "when do you want to enter?"

"Well, Papa, I've been thinking about that, too. I'd like to enter next month."

At first, Teresita's vocation was a bitter blow for Doctor Calixto Quevedo and his wife. How could they get along without their youngest daughter, who was only seventeen and so full of energy and enthusiasm?

But soon, with God's grace, Teresita's parents understood that her vocation was a blessing from God.

On February 23, 1947, Teresita Quevedo entered the Institute of the Carmelite Sisters of Charity, which was located in a little town just outside of Madrid.

Days at the novitiate turned into weeks and weeks into months. Before Teresita knew it, profession was not far away. But walking down the hall one day, she suddenly winced in pain. *Oh, well,* she thought, *maybe it's just another headache like the one I had yesterday.* However, the throbbing increased until Teresita could no longer concentrate on her work.

When she told the superior how severe her headache was, the superior sent her to the infirmary for some medication. Two days later, Doctor Quevedo was summoned to the novitiate.

He arrived within an hour and gave Teresita a thorough examination, discovering that his daughter had tubercular meningitis.

With anguish tearing at his heart, Doctor Quevedo told the Reverend Mother, "I fear my daughter will die in a matter of months. Not even the best care will prevent it. Usually patients are paralyzed, but in her case death isn't far off."

One morning the sister in charge of the infirmary walked over to her bedside and asked, "Sister, don't you feel a bit sad when you think of leaving everything you love?"

"Why should I, Sister?" Teresita replied. "Besides, I'm not really leaving everything I love. I have a Father in heaven who is waiting for me and a Mother who will come to bring me to God. I've always loved our Lady, and she is my greatest comfort now."

Smiling down into Teresita's glowing eyes, the other sister felt impelled to say, "Everyone here knows that you have an extraordinary love of our Lady. How did you acquire it?"

"All I did was try to do the little things perfectly. I've had to overcome many difficulties, and I have never done anything great in life, but I've found that Mary is a great means for reaching heaven. I have done everything for God through Mary. My gifts to Mary have been little ones. But, it's the little things in life that count."

As the sister-nurse resumed her infirmary duties, she thought about Teresita's words. Was it just a coincidence that especially on Saturdays and feasts of the Blessed Mother the sisters would be surprised to find their shoes "mysteriously" shined or their stockings suddenly mended? Although the sisters knew she was the culprit, Teresita never gave herself away. She would go quietly from room to room, leaving behind shoes polished to perfection, and then slip unnoticed into the laundry to darn a few pairs of black stockings before the wash would be divided.

The infirmarian recalled another episode.

One of Teresita's fellow novices had been bedridden in the infirmary. Worn out by a long illness, she wasn't talking much. She didn't want to read; she didn't even care to have the other sisters read to her. Whoever stayed with her had to be resigned to silence.

The superior wanted someone to spend at least the recreation period with the patient. She hoped for volunteers, but none was forthcoming . . . except Teresita. Right before the eagerly awaited recreation, she would ask, "Mother, could I spend recreation in the infirmary today?" The request always ended with "today," but the sister-nurse and the superior noticed that "today" became every day, for quite a while. The permission was always granted. And Teresita, delighted with her triumph, would hurry off.

That must have been quite a sacrifice for her, mused the sister-nurse. Teresita, so naturally joyful and exuberant, had looked forward to recreation more than all the other novices combined! She loved to chat and laugh, to enjoy the warm companionship and homey fun that bubbled up spontaneously among her sisters. Yet Teresita had sought out her quiet, suffering companion instead.

Her love for Mary played no small part in that victory. In her private notebook, Teresita had written, "May all who look at me, see you, O Mary!" And whether others knew of her resolution or not, it certainly wasn't hard to see the likeness of Mary mirrored in her joyful kindness.

Death drew near Teresita gradually. On Holy Saturday morning, April 8, 1950, pain racked every bone in her body, yet the young sister remained joyful and serene. When her father, Doctor Quevedo, came to visit her that morning, he realized that Teresita was on the verge of death. He thought back to when his beloved daughter had been a little girl. He could still hear her bursts of laughter and delight as she ran along the Spanish seacoast, chasing waves.

Then as he sat helplessly, watching her facial expression reflect the agony in her once vibrant body, he recalled an incident that had taken place a few summers before. At a swimming club a lifeguard approached to say, "Doctor Quevedo, your daughter is an outstanding swimmer and diver. Has she ever entered a diving contest?"

"Juan," the doctor replied, "if you have in mind what I suspect you do, I don't encourage you to ask Teresita about it. She already declined one of my friends last summer when he asked her to join in the diving contests."

Juan thanked Doctor Quevedo and then went down to the beach to see if he could find Teresita. Well, he thought, no girl has yet refused me. I just don't understand how a girl like Teresita could say no when she thinks of the trophies she would easily win.

Minutes later he ran into Teresita. "May I speak with you for a minute?" he inquired. "I won't take much of your time, Señorita Quevedo. I know you might be in a hurry. . . ."

"No, Juan," Teresita said. "I'm not in a hurry. What do you need?"

"Well, Teresita, I was speaking with your father not long ago, and I understand that you are an excellent swimmer. Why don't you take part in the diving contests that are coming up soon? None of the participants in your age bracket can match your speed or technique as a diver. Think of the honor it will give you and of the glory it will bring your parents!"

Teresita thought a moment before she answered. Then she said, "Juan, will it bring honor and glory to the Mother of God?"

For a second Juan was speechless. Teresita's decision hung upon the answer he was now searching for.

"Well, Teresita, let's leave her—I mean the Blessed Mother— out of this."

"Okay, Juan, if that's what you really want … but I'll stay with our Lady."

Now Doctor Quevedo felt helpless and alone as he looked at Teresita, who was dying of a disease that medicine could not cure. It took all the courage he had to just stand there and watch Teresita draw nearer and nearer to death. But thinking over her past life and her great devotion to Mary, he began to pray to the Blessed Mother for the strength he needed to accept God's will in his daughter's regard. When the phone rang the next morning, the doctor answered in a natural tone of voice. The superior asked him to come as soon as possible. Teresita had passed to eternity. When Doctor and Señora Quevedo reached the convent, the superior related the details. An aura of joy filled the air as she spoke …

Teresita had been sinking rapidly. The white bed that had become an altar trembled from the pain that racked her body, and she gave no sign of consciousness. Suddenly, she opened her eyes, and her usually soft voice filled the room:

"My Mother, Mary, come for me! Bring me back to heaven with you!"

The community was summoned and filed prayerfully into the room, which seemed more like a cathedral than a sickroom. The sisters knelt around Teresita's bed. She was quiet, almost motionless except for the gentle rise and fall of the sheets as she labored to breathe.

Then it happened, like the bursting crescendo in a hymn of victory. The dying nun opened her eyes, and a radiant smile lit her face for the last time:

"Oh, how beautiful! O Mary, how beautiful you are!"

Those who knew her well all agreed that "Mary was her life." And Mary had come to lead her into the dawn of life eternal.

"Death has been swallowed up in victory.
'Where, O death, is your victory?
'Where, O death, is your sting?'"

(1 Cor 15:54–55)

Teresita Quevedo had won the victory.

Personal Challenge

In the spirit of Venerable Teresita Quevedo, how can I allow Mary to lead me to seek God's glory, even in the small things of my life?

Prayer

Dear Jesus, we ask you to give us the insight you gave Teresita Quevedo to realize the importance of life. At a young age she was inspired to offer her life to you through your Mother Mary. She knew the secret of pleasing you is found in living with your Mother, imitating her virtues, sharing her intentions. Make this desire for holiness a part of our vocation in life as well, no matter what path we follow. Amen.

Facts About Her Life

~::~ Her full name was Maria Teresa Josefina Justina Gonzalez-Quevedo y Cadarso. She was the third child of Dr. Calixto Gonzalez Quevedo and his wife, Maria del Carmen Cadarso.

~::~ Teresita was baptized by Father Ignatius Navarro, chaplain to King Alfonso XIII, at Saint Francis Church across from the Royal Palace.

~:~ A lover of fashion, she was once voted "best dressed" in her class.

~:~ Her interests included dancing, swimming, tennis, basketball (team captain), and the Marian Sodality.

~:~ Four of her aunts were Carmelites of Charity, and two uncles were Jesuits.

~:~ She entered the novitiate of the Carmelites of Charity on February 23, 1948.

~:~ She desired to be a missionary to China.

~:~ She predicted that she would be in heaven for the declaration of the dogma of Mary's Assumption into Heaven, which occurred on November 1, 1950.

~:~ She was allowed to anticipate her profession of vows due to her illness.

~:~ She was sometimes called Tere.

~:~ She wrote a "Code or Ten Commandments of Amiability."

In Her Own Words

"May all who look at me see you, O Mary."

Reader's Guide for Venerable Teresita, page 184.

BLESSED ARE THE
MERCIFUL, FOR THEY
WILL RECEIVE MERCY.

Saint Frances Xavier Cabrini

"What About China?"

BORN: July 15, 1850, in Lombardy, Italy

DIED: December 22, 1917, in Chicago, of malaria

FEAST DAY: November 13

CANONIZED: June 7, 1946, by Pope Pius XII

PATRON: immigrants, emigrants, hospital administrators

What was Mother Cabrini thinking about that evening in December 1917 as she prepared little parcels of candy for poor children of the neighborhood? To her sisters she had announced that "this Christmas must be a special one." Perhaps she thought of all the preceding Christmases or of all the little ones she had cherished through the years.

Francesca Cabrini was born July 15, 1850, in the small farming community of Sant'Angelo Lodigiano, Lombardy, the youngest of the eleven children of Agostino and Stella (Oldini)

Cabrini. Cecchina, as she was affectionately called, was born prematurely to a couple who had suffered the loss of several children already. She was beautiful and beloved. As she grew, Francesca delighted in listening to her father read from *The Annals of the Propagation of the Faith*. Her little heart absorbed the tales of the great missionaries, and she longed to follow them to far-off places. These dreams almost led to disaster one day as Cecchina placed her little paper boat full of missionaries in a stream and sent them off to China. She was leaning over the embankment to watch as they swirled away when her foot slipped and she tumbled into the fast-moving stream. Floundering about and gulping water, the little missionary was on the verge of panic when a stranger lifted her out. Relatives had come running when they lost sight of her. "Cecchina," they cried. "You're soaking wet."

"I fell in the water," she whimpered.

Eyeing the moving stream, they asked, "But how did you get out by yourself?"

"A man picked me up," she replied, shivering from the cold.

"But there is no one anywhere to be seen," they exclaimed to one other. It was concluded that this "someone" must have been her guardian angel. Meanwhile, the little girl was bundled in someone's coat and brought quickly home.

As a young woman, Francesca kept her ideal before her. "I will go to the missions. My heart is set on spreading the Gospel to the people of China," she would repeat. She enrolled in the boarding school of the Daughters of the Sacred Heart to prepare for a teaching degree, which she obtained in 1868. Consecrating herself totally to God as a religious now held sway over her heart, and she asked to enter the community. The superior replied, "No, Francesca. We think very highly of you, but your health will not support this way of life. However, we believe you are destined to honor the Sacred Heart in another way." Francesca turned away, teary-eyed. Later she applied to the Canossian Sisters, but they also told her that God must have other plans for her.

Indeed, God did have other plans, but sadly, they began with the sudden deaths of both of her beloved parents. For now, Francesca felt she could be a missionary in the confines of Sant'Angelo, so she helped her older sister Rosa with the school she had begun and with nursing the neighborhood's poor and shut-ins. During an outbreak of smallpox, Francesca fell ill but soon recovered through Rosa's loving care. Despite this further health setback, Francesca took her first steps toward the missions in 1871 when her pastor invited her to take a position as a substitute teacher in nearby Vidardo. For two years she diligently taught her young charges not only to read and write but also to love and serve their God.

The pastor of Vidardo, Don Serrati, was pleased with her abilities and suggested that she assist some ladies who were running an orphanage in Codogno, where he had recently transferred. It seems the ladies who donated the home and finances for the orphanage were not very practical; things needed turning around. Don Serrati gave her two weeks to perform this "miracle" at the House of Providence. Francesca did bring about the transformation, and the pastor invited her to stay. She was happy to agree, but the ladies who were operating the house were not so pleased. Two months later the priest was inspired to invite the group of women to don a habit and form themselves into a religious community. For the next six years the group lived their new life in great hope and great tension, and in September 1877 they made their profession of vows. Francesca added the name Saveria (Xavier) to her own in honor of her favorite missionary saint. Suddenly the joy of the occasion turned to apprehension as the bishop looked at the newly professed group and announced, "I have decided to appoint Sister Francesca as your superior." Certainly, the young religious, only twenty-seven years old, never expected this, but she saw God's will in the bishop's wishes and obeyed. However, what began that day came to a sudden end in 1880 when the bishop was forced to suppress the House of Providence and disband the sisters. This was not Mother Francesca's fault at all. In fact, the other sisters had witnessed the harassment she had to endure from the original "foundresses" of the House. Nothing pleased them, and they went out of their way to criticize and threaten their new superior. And so, the bishop invited Mother Francesca to begin her dream of a missionary community, along with several of the sisters and some former students. They found an abandoned monastery in Codogno and thus began the Missionaries of the Sacred Heart of Jesus. The blessing of God was definitely on this new institute, which grew rapidly. Membership soon increased, for many young women were inspired both by the name of the new institute and by its spirit. Soon Mother Cabrini established five convents in Lombardy and then set her sights on Rome. "If we can open a house in Rome, we will be in the heart of the Church," she thought.

Standing in the presence of the cardinal vicar of Rome, Lucido Parocchi, Mother Cabrini stated her desires. "Your Eminence, we would like to receive recognition of our institute and your permission to begin our missionary work here in Rome."

The cardinal's welcoming smile turned to a frown as he replied, "Mother, your congregation is very new. Others are still awaiting this permission. Return to Codogno and your work there." Stifling tears, Mother Cabrini and her companion had no choice but to leave.

She was inspired, however, to return soon after and ask permission to stay at least until the institute's constitutions were approved. Cardinal Parocchi agreed and promised to ask the Holy Father about their request. In October, the cardinal called for them and asked, "Mother, are you ready to obey?"

"Yes, certainly," she replied.

"Then," the cardinal proceeded with a slight smile, "you will open not one house, but two." This wonderful surprise from the Lord led to another opportunity of grace. While in Rome, Mother Cabrini met Bishop Giovanni Battista Scalabrini, founder of the Missionary Institute of Saint Charles, who ministered to Italians living overseas. He told her about the needs of their countrymen who had emigrated to the United States. They faced great trials, and many were abandoning the practice of their faith. Certainly she would find a fertile field there for the Gospel. In her mind Mother Cabrini kept asking, "But what about China?" She still had to get approval to begin missionary life in earnest. When she finally was granted a meeting with Pope Leo XIII, she told him about her great desire to go to China. He asked many questions about her plans for the new institute. Then, looking at her expectant face, he said, "No, Mother! You must not go east, but west! Go to America. Evangelize among the Italians who are living there. That will be your mission." The Sacred Heart had spoken through the Pope, and Mother Cabrini believed this was indeed the will of God. So in a very short time she, along with six of her daughters, boarded a ship to New York.

Although Bishop Scalabrini had said that Bishop Michael

Corrigan of New York would be expecting the sisters, he actually was not. When the sisters arrived, he unceremoniously suggested they should take the same ship back to Italy. "No," said Mother Cabrini firmly. "Your Excellency, we have come with letters from the Holy Father. We must stay." So Bishop Corrigan agreed, and accommodations were found with the Sisters of Charity. The great missionary life of Mother Cabrini had begun.

In an unbelievably short time, the Missionaries of the Sacred Heart began schools, orphanages, catechetical programs, and other works of charity in various places. Bishop Corrigan soon came to love and to count on these courageous women. He asked Mother Cabrini to start a hospital for the poor. At first she declined, saying that nursing was not part of their mission, but then she came back, stood before his desk, and said yes. The bishop asked, "Mother, what caused this change?"

Simply, she explained: "I had a dream in which I saw Mary caring for the sick. I asked her what she was doing. She replied, 'What you refused to do.' And so, I understand that this too is part of God's plan."

Not knowing anything beyond her early days of assisting Rosa in nursing the sick of Sant'Angelo, Mother Cabrini began in faith. Soon doctors and other medical personnel volunteered their services, and Columbus Hospital was born. In the years that followed, Mother Cabrini traveled not only across the United States opening schools, hospitals, and orphanages, but she also made her way to Nicaragua, Panama, France, Brazil, Spain, Argentina, and England, establishing the Missionaries of the Sacred Heart to serve God's people and give him glory.

And how much glory God received through the boundless love of this missionary heart! The years passed, and now

Christmas was approaching in 1917. Mother Cabrini recalled all those Christmases in the past when she had given so many gifts to the Heart of Jesus and received so many in return. Now, God had prepared a final gift for this generous soul who had given herself as a mother to so many. Mother Cabrini had been feeling tired this morning and was now praying in her room. When a sister came to call her for the midday meal, she found Mother had locked her door. Returning a little later, the sister was shocked to find the door unlocked and Mother sitting peacefully in her chair. She had been quietly called home to God.

Mother Cabrini's legacy to the Church is one of unstinting love, which translates itself into mercy. Through her efforts and those of her sisters, not only Italian immigrants but persons of every nationality and need found the love of Christ in search of them, ready to assist them in their struggles, giving them the hope to begin again.

She was canonized in 1946, just twenty-nine years after her death. One word can define this great woman of faith: *missionary*. Saint Frances Xavier Cabrini herself offers the definition of a missionary, which is a resumé of her own incredible life: "What is a missionary? To me a missionary is an uncompromising lover of the Sacred Heart. She is his candle that radiates light while she consumes her life embracing everything—labors, joys and pains—for the salvation of all people."

Personal Challenge

How can I, like Saint Frances Xavier Cabrini, go out of my comfort zone to assist people who are less fortunate than myself and make the love of Jesus present to them?

Prayer

Saint Frances Xavier Cabrini, mother of all who are uprooted from their homelands, who seek a new and better life in unknown lands, help us open our hearts to the immigrants of our day. Like you, may we love all people, no matter their race, religion, or country of origin, with the same love that you learned from the Sacred Heart of Jesus. Through your intercession we ask the strength and ingenuity to show that love in works of mercy toward those who suffer material or spiritual want. Amen.

Facts About Her Life

~:~ In her twenty-eight years as a missionary, she founded sixty-seven institutions in the United States, Argentina, Brazil, Spain, England, France, Nicaragua, and Panama.

~:~ Many miraculous and prophetic things occurred throughout her life.

~:~ She wrote extensively to her sisters during her travels.

~:~ She was buried in West Park, New York, but her body was later transferred to the shrine at Mother Cabrini High School in New York City.

~:~ She is the first American citizen to be proclaimed a saint.

~:~ One miracle for her canonization was the simultaneous cure of a man from three serious illnesses; the other was the instantaneous cure of another man's foot ailment.

~:~ She was named "Italian Immigrant of the Century" in 1952.

~:~ Her image is found in many places, including the bronze doors of Saint Patrick's Cathedral in New York, the National

Shrine of the Immaculate Conception in Washington, D.C., the museum on Liberty Island, New York (home of the Statue of Liberty), and Saint Peter's Basilica in Vatican City.

~:~ Although she was deathly afraid of water, she crossed the ocean thirty times.

In Her Own Words

"That which, being women, we are not allowed to do on a large scale, such as helping to solve important social problems, is being done in our little sphere in every state and in every city where our houses have been opened."

Reader's Guide for Saint Frances Cabrini, page 186.

Saint Martin de Porres

A Man Among Men

Born: December 9, 1579, in Lima, Peru

Died: November 3, 1639, in Lima

Feast Day: November 3

Canonized: May 6, 1962, by Pope Saint John XXIII

Patron: social justice, racial harmony, barbers, surgeons, nurses, innkeepers, Peru, animals, poor people, public education, television, Dominican tertiaries, public health

November 3, 1639—seemingly a day like any other. In Lima, Peru, however, it was a day of tragedy and triumph—of tragedy because Peru had lost one of her best-loved sons; of triumph because this son was Lima's glory.

In a small room of the Dominican monastery of the Holy Rosary, the commanding voice of the Archbishop of Mexico City broke through the stillness:

"Let us learn from the edifying death of Brother Martin how to die well. It is a most important and most difficult lesson."

The body of Martin de Porres was laid out before the main altar in the monastery chapel. Then the friars opened the doors of the chapel to permit Martin's closest friends—the poor, the homeless, the old, and the sick—to bid him a final farewell.

As the body grew colder and more rigid, a disappointed confrere, who had hoped for a miracle that would indicate Martin's holiness, went near and affectionately chided him, "Why is your body stiff and rigid, Brother Martin? Ask God to show his almighty power by permitting it to remain lifelike." Within a few moments, a fragrance of roses and lilies arose from the coffin, and Martin's rigid body relaxed and grew soft.

Now the crowds could not be held back. The people cut to shreds Brother Martin's habit, which had to be replaced several times. Numerous authenticated miracles took place.

Martin's story had begun quite differently just sixty years earlier.

He was the son of a Spanish nobleman and a free Black woman. His father deserted the family shortly after the birth of Martin's younger sister, Juana. Unfortunately, like other children, Martin learned at a very early age just how bitter life can be.

"Half-breed," people whispered as he passed the more fashionable quarters of Lima on his way home to the poorest section of the city. But Martin's bright face never clouded, and his happy disposition never changed. He smiled and waved to passersby as he skipped through busy city streets. Martin's job as a delivery boy added a few coins to his mother's meager earnings. By the time he was eight, he had learned where he could find the best buys.

Shopkeepers and open-air merchants knew that the food Martin bought at the market was not all for himself, nor only for his mother and sister. In fact, Martin often gave away more than half of everything he had to his beggar friends. Then he would turn to old benefactors who would refill Martin's basket and send him on his way with a warning, "Remember, go straight home this time."

But one day someone asked, "Do you know who is on the ship that docked this morning?"

What a strange question, Martin thought. "Sailors, I guess," he replied.

"No, Martin, not just sailors. Your father, Don Juan de Porres, is on that boat."

"Don Juan—my father—is in Lima now?" Martin raced toward home so fast that his neighbors looked to see who was chasing him.

He dashed inside the house, dropped his basket on the table, and quickly glanced around. He caught his breath and then announced seriously, "Juana, our father is here in Lima, and he is coming to see us."

"Our father?" Juana responded, wide-eyed. "Do you mean we have a father, too?"

"Yes, and we'll have to tidy up the house and put on our church clothes."

In the space of a few weeks, great changes took place in Martin's life. He and Juana went to Ecuador, where they lived with their father's uncle, Don Diego. Used to lacking even the barest necessities, the children were overwhelmed by the lifestyle of their wealthy relatives.

Martin remained in Ecuador almost three years, but he never forgot his poor mother, whom he had left behind in Lima. Although the boy was grateful for all that his father and Don

Diego were doing for him, his heart ached when he thought of how lonely his mother must be.

After returning to Lima, the youth took up a heavy round of prayer, work, study, and visits to the sick. He was apprenticed to a barber-surgeon and learned his profession well. He spent whatever money he made on the poor, and he again became a regular visitor to the marketplace, now as the benefactor.

A year or two later, the keeper of the house where Martin was staying was abruptly awakened before sunrise by a loud noise in the street. As she passed Martin's room, she noticed a sliver of light under the door.

"He must have fallen asleep studying," she said to herself. "I'd better wake him up and make him go to bed."

The landlady knocked on the door, but there was no answer. She tried a second time. Still no answer. Then the door swung open. She gasped in astonishment. Wrapped in a state of ecstasy, Martin was kneeling in front of a crucifix, his whole body enveloped in a bright light. She closed the door again and thanked God for having given her the privilege of lodging a person so dear to him. More and more, one could hear talk in the streets of people whom Martin had helped in strange and almost miraculous ways.

Another year passed, and Martin longed to do something more for God. After praying for light and guidance, he presented himself to the prior of the Dominican Monastery of the Holy Rosary. He told the priest that he would like to live at the monastery as a lay helper.

A few days later, sixteen-year-old Martin said goodbye to all his friends, packed his medical instruments, and left for the Dominican monastery. Shortly after he arrived, he was assigned to work in the infirmary, where he accomplished wonders for souls as well as bodies. When Martin's father heard that his son had such a lowly position, he demanded that he be accepted at least as a professed brother. "But, Señor de Porres, that was our wish as well, but your son said that he preferred simply to serve." Only later, when Martin was twenty-four, did his superiors persuade him to take vows. He made his novitiate and donned the habit of the Dominican brother. Unknown to most, he also took up wearing a heavy chain around his waist under the habit and regularly did other severe penances. Martin slept very little and often gave away his own meal yet seemed to have unrelenting energy. He performed jobs normally assigned to several brothers. He was in charge of supplying food, caring for the clothing, nursing the sick, cleaning the monastery, and many other duties.

The amount of work he continued to do was miraculous in itself. But the countless and inexplicable cures he obtained were even more miraculous. One of these cures involved a certain Brother Francis, who was tempted to abandon his vocation. He was scheming to secretly leave the monastery to take up a government post. The young man went about his duties as if all were well. Approaching the dining room for the evening meal, Martin, who knew the brother really had a vocation, stepped in front of him and whispered, "Are you really going to leave your vocation to become a bookkeeper for the city? That will never do!"

That evening Brother Francis went to bed with a high fever. When he recovered, he tried again to leave. The fever felled him a second time, but recovering he set his mind to depart the monastery. Now, the third time, the fever put him in bed with pleurisy. He struggled to breathe. The superiors, afraid a companion might give him some remedy that would cause greater harm, locked Brother Francis in his room. But God sent in Martin. Just after midnight, as Francis lay mournfully in bed, he sensed someone near him. "Who is it?" he rasped. Then he recognized Martin's smiling face. Martin said nothing but set down the brazier he always carried and placed sprigs of rosemary on the coals. As the sweet fragrance filled the room, Martin began attending to Francis. He washed him and changed his nightclothes. He then wrapped him in a warm blanket and put him back to bed.

"The door is locked, Brother Martin. How did you come in?" the young man struggled to ask.

The answer ended any discussion. "This is not something to try to understand, my son."

"Will I die?" was his next question.

"Do you want to?" Martin asked.

"No," came the quick reply.

"Then you will not die," said his visitor, vanishing as silently as he came. The next morning found Francis restored to health and convinced of his vocation.

Martin not only took care of his confreres, but he also cared for sick people of the city. Martin sometimes even gave them his own bed. Once he found a man outside the monastery who was bleeding and terribly dirty, and Martin brought him in for care. When the man recovered and was sent back home, the brother in charge of laundry accosted Martin. "Look at these sheets. They are filthy. We'll never get them clean again!"

"Some elbow grease along with soap and water will do the trick, my brother," Martin replied. "You know that will work on our clothes, but our souls require tears and penance to be clean of our thoughtlessness."

Martin's concern was not limited to his fellow human beings; he is also known for his love of animals. He did not search out furry friendships, but animals seemed to sense he was their friend and protector. Dogs often appeared after fights or run-ins with impatient masters. He would clean and dress their wounds and have the poor beasts stay in his room, telling them to be quiet and behave well. When they were sufficiently healed, he would send them off with a good word.

Martin is famous for his kindness to the mice. Once the little pests got into the monastery linen closet and feasted on the cloth. The brothers were furious and wanted to put poison around. Brother Martin interceded. "They can't go into a dining room and find meals prepared as we do, but they still have to eat." He went to the closet and caught one of the little vandals. Holding it in his hand, he put forward a plan. "My little friend, you must not eat the things set aside for the sick. Assemble your family every day at the far side of the garden. I will bring you food." The tiny mouse must have agreed because after that the linen closet was not disturbed. The little band of mice arrived each day for the meal set out by Martin in the garden.

So much charity, so many signs and wonders. Martin had labored hard and long, with never a complaint or a moment of respite. He was a man among men, big enough to overcome prejudice and humble enough to hide the special powers he wielded. He was a man who lived solely for God, as the instrument of his mercy.

Personal Challenge

In the spirit of Martin de Porres, what is one thing I can ask of Jesus to show me what he wants of me as his disciple?

Prayer

Dear Saint Martin de Porres, we look to you with such admiration, not so much because you were able to work wonders, but because you were a true man of God. You were a man of intense yet tender prayer. You gave yourself generously to the work at hand and gave your own time and talent to the needs of others. It did not matter to you if you were serving the rich or the poor, your brothers or strangers, the kind or the impertinent. We see this in your example, but help us find this same merciful spirit in our own hearts. Amen.

Facts About His Life

~::~ He was the son of Juan de Porres, a noble Spanish gentleman who later became governor of Panama, and a free Black woman named Ana Velasquez.

~::~ When Martin was eight years old, his father took him and his sister to Ecuador for schooling.

~::~ At sixteen, he became a "donado," or lay helper, in the Third Order of Saint Dominic.

~::~ He desired to be a missionary martyr.

~::~ He was known as Martin the Charitable.

~::~ He possessed exceptional gifts: bilocation, elevation, infused knowledge, miraculous healings, prophecy, and the power to raise the dead.

~::~ He was a vegetarian.

~::~ He established a hospital, an orphanage, and an animal shelter in Lima.

~:~ He was a contemporary of Saint Rose of Lima, Saint John Macias, and Saint Turibius of Mogrovejo.

~:~ He was known to contemporaries as "father of charity" because he so inspired people to share in the care of other people.

~:~ Letters permitting the opening of his cause went down in a shipwreck but were recovered unscathed.

~:~ The miracles for his canonization were the instant cure of an inoperable intestinal blockage in an elderly woman and the complete restoration of the crushed foot of a child.

~:~ A scent of roses accompanied his exhumed body to a new tomb in 1664.

In His Own Words

(Having been berated by one of his patients) "I must take better care of him and love him more because he knows me better than anyone else."

Reader's Guide for Saint Martin, page 188.

BLESSED ARE THE
PURE IN HEART, FOR
THEY WILL SEE GOD.

Saint Kateri Tekakwitha

Mystic of the Wilderness

BORN: 1656 in Ossernenon, NY, United States
DIED: April 17, 1680, in Kahnawake, Canada
FEAST DAY: July 14 in the United States, April 17 in Canada
CANONIZED: October 21, 2012, by Pope Benedict XVI
PATRON: Native Americans, ecology and the environment, orphans,
   purity

Tekakwitha watched the happy faces around the fire inside the longhouse. For some reason, even her aunt looked pleased. Her uncle, Chief Iowerano, caught her glance as he smoked on his pipe. Her stomach tightened with tension at his knowing eyes, although his face remained expressionless. Something was going on. Was she the only one not to know? She scanned the faces in the longhouse and caught a glimpse of the impassive face of their guest, a young warrior—this young man did not seem caught up in the excitement of a secret.

Behind her, her aunt motioned to the young man to sit down beside Tekakwitha and gave Tekakwitha the bowl of sagamite

107

(hominy stew) to pass to him. Suddenly, Tekakwitha's throat closed. Her aunt was trying to trick her into marriage—an exchange of gifts meant betrothal—and if she hadn't realized it in time, she would have had to marry him! She dropped the bowl, got to her feet, and fled the longhouse.

As she left, she glanced back at her uncle. He did not seem surprised, only disappointed. Tekakwitha was shaking so badly that she stumbled her way out of the palisade into the privacy of the forest. Tears streamed down her face. She was not afraid of her uncle's displeasure. What he thought best for her was irreconcilable with her own desires, and that had soured much of the joy in their kinship. Yet, she knew that he loved her and valued her diligence in farming and around the longhouse. And her aunt's deception did not anger her as much as frighten her. Tekakwitha had almost been tricked into a marriage that she had made clear to her family she could never accept!

The young man himself was not the objection. Tekakwitha simply did not want to get married even though it was unheard-of for a young maiden to remain single. She had gone along with some of the customs for young women only to please her aunts and uncle. She had obeyed them in everything except their urging her to marry. Even in the face of ridicule and cruelty, she stubbornly refused.

Tekakwitha had just two desires: the first was to continue to serve her family as she always had. The second she dared not share with anyone. She desperately wanted to become a Christian as her mother had been. Ever since she had met the Black Robes and heard them speak about God, she had been drawn to their loving God, Rawanniio. If she married, she would probably lose the chance to become a Christian and dedicate her life to this

God she longed to know. The Black Robes had been living at her village for some time, but she hadn't sought them out to ask for instruction because it would displease her uncle. He didn't like any of the French, including the Black Robes. He remembered, as Tekakwitha did, that French soldiers had burned down their village ten years ago, and they had had to flee with nothing, barely surviving the winter.

If Tekakwitha could just speak with one of the Black Robes! She was drawn to their goodness and their desire for peace. She knew that they did not approve of the cannibalism and torture of war prisoners that so disturbed Tekakwitha. But she only knew fragments of prayers. And she had so many questions!

Tekakwitha quieted her sobs and offered a prayer. "Rawanniio, if you want me to know you, help me!"

Some days later, Tekakwitha was sitting in the longhouse all alone. The other women were working in the fields, but she had injured her foot and had been left behind for the longhouse chores. She didn't mind. The bright sunlight hurt her eyes, making it impossible to see. In the dim light of the longhouse fire, she could continue her skilled beadwork.

As she leaned over her work, someone stepped into the entrance of the longhouse and spoke in the silence. "Is someone here?" an unfamiliar voice asked. Tekakwitha's breath stopped. God had answered her prayer!

"Yes, Father," she said calmly. But her heart was beating rapidly.

He walked over and looked down at her. "You know who I am?" he asked.

"Oh, yes," she breathed. "You are a Black Robe who can tell me about Rawanniio!"

The Black Robe seemed surprised, then he sat down by the fire and started telling her about his Christian God of love. As he spoke, he noticed how she paid close attention, eagerly drinking in every word.

"Why don't you come to the mission?" he asked as he got up to leave. "You can join us for prayer and instruction."

Tekakwitha explained as simply as she could. "My uncle, Chief Iowerano, would be displeased."

"Have you asked him?" the Black Robe asked.

"No," Tekakwitha said.

The Black Robe nodded, turned away, then turned back. "I will pray for you," he said. Then he left.

Tekakwitha's heart leaped for joy. The Black Robe would pray for her! As he walked away, she thought, "My uncle is displeased I do not choose to marry, but he has given up trying to force me. Maybe . . . this will displease my uncle, but he will let me do as I ask?"

Tekakwitha was right. Reluctantly, Iowerano gave Tekakwitha permission to be instructed, probably suspecting that in this, too, Tekakwitha's determination would not fail. As she got to know the Black Robes better, Tekakwitha confided her story to Father de Lamberville.

Tekakwitha was born in April 1656 in the Mohawk settlement of Ossernenon, located in what is now Auriesville, New York. She was the daughter of the Mohawk warrior chief Tsaniton-gowa and his kind and gentle wife, Kahontake—an Algonquin woman captured during a Mohawk raid on her settlement. Kahontake's goodness irresistibly attracted the attention of Tsaniton-gowa, who brought her to Ossernenon not as a slave, but as his wife.

As Tsaniton-gowa's wife, Kahontake enjoyed complete freedom, except that she could not practice Christianity openly. When God blessed their marriage with a baby girl, Kahontake secretly taught her child a knowledge of Rawanniio and the desire to practice Christian virtue.

But smallpox struck the village when Tekakwitha was only four years old. Both her parents and her younger brother died. Tekakwitha, too, contracted smallpox. Anastasia, a Christian friend of her mother's, nursed her back to health. However, Tekakwitha was scarred on her face and left partially blind, so painfully sensitive to bright sunlight that she covered her head with a blanket when she was outdoors.

Her uncle, Iowerano, now a new chief, had been as devastated as she by the loss. He had picked her up and carried her off to his own longhouse, adopting her as his own and placing her in the care of her two aunts.

As Tekakwitha grew, so did her skill at beadwork and her dependability in domestic affairs. Iowerano was very pleased with his niece in many ways, though she sometimes puzzled him. She was not like other girls her age: she kept apart and silent, and she didn't like to go to dances or village gatherings. He didn't know if this was due to her inability to see clearly in sunlight, her pockmarked face, her natural shyness, or the suffering she had undergone as a child.

When she was free, Tekakwitha loved to run off into the forest to pray. She longed to know Rawanniio and begged for his help. The words and examples of her good mother had made a lasting impression on her, an impression time intensified rather than softened. Finally, when missionaries came to the village, they found this unique young Mohawk maiden, although unbaptized and uninstructed, deeply Christian in her manner of speaking and living.

After a year of instruction, Tekakwitha managed to prevail on her uncle once more: he gave her permission to be baptized! On Easter morning, April 18, 1676, she received Baptism and the Christian name Katherine, which the converts pronounced "Kateri." The next few months, Kateri spent her days working busily in her uncle's house and helping the needy of the village, including the aged and the sick. But some in the village, including her aunt and other relatives, grew suspicious of Kateri's resistance to marriage and the way she practiced her faith. Calumny, taunts, threats, and hostility soon became a daily part of Kateri's life. At last, a young warrior wearing war paint stopped her and pretended he was going to kill her, raising a tomahawk over her head. Eyes lowered, she awaited the blow, showing no signs of fear. The man ran off, impressed with her courage.

Father de Lamberville realized that it was too dangerous for Kateri to remain among her people. He suggested that she flee to Saint Francis Xavier, the Christian native village in Kahnawake near Montreal, where Kateri's mother's friend Anastasia and an adopted sister lived. Kateri resisted this plan for quite a while. She did not want to leave her people, nor break her uncle's heart. Finally, Kateri's brother-in-law made the trip to visit her village with the secret purpose of rescuing Kateri. His descriptions of the "Praying Village" where Christian converts lived peaceably together so appealed to her that she decided to take the risk. That night, several young men guided Kateri out of the village and hid her in the forest.

Terribly hurt and angry, Iowerano went searching for her. It was rumored that he threatened to kill Kateri for her betrayal.

Yet, when he met one of the young men getting supplies in Fort Orange, he merely greeted him and went on. Kateri, who was hiding in the woods, would never see her uncle again.

After an arduous three-week journey, Kateri and her companions arrived at Kahnawake. The village was full of the fervor of new converts, and the Christian women happily welcomed her, including her mother's old friend Anastasia. Three months after her arrival, on Christmas Day, Kateri made her first Holy Communion. She impressed everyone with her deep prayer, unceasing kindness, and great desire to do penance and offer sacrifices for the enlightenment of her people. Kateri was greatly devoted to Jesus in the Eucharist. At every moment free of work or service, Kateri could be found at the chapel, usually arriving earlier than the priests in the morning. She also loved to pray out in the woods, where she would carve a cross in one of the trees to make her own little chapel.

Even here in Kahnawake, Kateri soon found herself being urged to find a good husband. But Kateri resisted any suggestion to marry. On a visit to Montreal, she had seen the Religious Hospitallers of Saint Joseph and had finally understood her vocation. She felt called, like the sisters, to dedicate her whole life to Jesus. When her sister-in-law and her mother's old friend pressured her unfairly one day, she went to see Father Cholenec, the village Black Robe who was directing her. Resolutely she told him of her decision to renounce marriage in order to love only Christ. On March 25, 1679, the Feast of the Annunciation, Kateri confirmed her resolution with a vow of virginity. Kateri also wanted to start a community of sisters for native women, but the priest discouraged her. Perhaps he could see how her strength was failing. Or perhaps he felt it was too soon after her conversion.

Barely one year later, the young maiden lay on her death-bed. She had never been strong, her penances had weakened her, and she caught a persistent fever. On Wednesday of Holy Week, April 17, 1680, Kateri went to the embrace of Jesus, whom she had loved and for whom she had suffered so much. She was twenty-four years old. Fifteen minutes after her death, Father Cholenec was startled by the change that came over the young woman's scarred face. The pockmarks disappeared, and her face became radiant and completely unblemished. After death, this simple, pure Mohawk-Algonquin woman would be recognized for who she was—a mystic of the North American wilderness.

Personal Challenge

In the spirit of Kateri Tekakwitha, what is one action you can take to better reflect how your body is a temple of the Holy Spirit?

Prayer

Saint Kateri Tekakwitha, lover of Jesus, the secret of your life is that you allowed the Good News of God's love to transform you. Your courage, your love for your people, and your purity of life were nurtured by your special devotion to Jesus in the Eucharist and on the Cross. You have been called "mystic of the wilderness." Pray for me, that my love for Christ may grow, that I may respect the sacredness of God's creation, and that I may discover and faithfully live what God wants. Amen.

Facts About Her Life

~::~ Born of a Catholic Algonquin mother and a Mohawk father, she was orphaned at age four.

~::~ Kateri Tekakwitha was a small woman, probably only about four and a half feet tall.

~::~ Left scarred and partially blind by smallpox, Kateri Tekakwitha suffered from poor health all her life.

~::~ "Tekakwitha" means "one who moves things," which some have assumed means that she put things in order. But most likely her name was given to her by her uncle because smallpox left her partially blind, and she used her hands to feel her way around. One possible translation of her name is "she who pushes with her hands."

~::~ "Kateri Tekakwitha" is correctly pronounced in Mohawk: Gah-deh-LEE (Kateri) Deh-gah-GWEE-tah (Tekakwitha).

~::~ She began instruction in Christianity in 1675, when she was nineteen years old.

~::~ She was baptized Easter Sunday, April 18, 1676 (in her home village).

~::~ Because she wouldn't work on Sunday, her family wouldn't allow her to eat all day.

~::~ She tolerated the ridicule and abuse from her family and people in her village because she knew they couldn't understand her conversion.

~::~ Kateri traveled more than two hundred miles on foot and by canoe to the Mission of Saint Francis Xavier, a settlement of

Christian Native Americans where she could safely live her faith.

~:~ She received her First Communion on Christmas Day, 1677.

~:~ On March 25, 1679, she made a vow of perpetual virginity—the first Native American woman known to consecrate her virginity to God.

~:~ She wanted to found a community of religious sisters for Native American women, but the Jesuits discouraged her from doing so.

~:~ She died at the young age of twenty-four, her poor health weakened by her fasting and other penances.

In Her Own Words

"Who will teach me what is most agreeable to God, so that I may do it?"

Reader's Guide for Saint Kateri, page 190.

Blessed Marie-Clémentine Anuarite Nengapeta

Sister Among Sisters

BORN: November 29, 1939, in Wamba, Belgian Congo

DIED: December 1, 1964, in Isiro, Zaire (now Democratic Republic of the Congo)

FEAST DAY: December 1

BEATIFIED: August 15, 1985

PATRON: the well-loved patron of young people in Africa

Sister Marie-Clémentine Anuarite smiled as she passed the fruit salad to Sister Andrée. Today her community, the Sisters of the Holy Family, were celebrating a feast day for Sister Andrée and herself, and it was so good to see the other sisters laugh. Earlier in the month, they had heard troubling rumors that Simba rebel forces were on the move. Since the Congo had gained independence four years earlier, there had been unpredictable spurts of violence and destruction. Times of celebration such as these had become even more precious.

The noise of a truck suddenly drowned out the sisters' laughter. At first, they were not alarmed, but then drunken soldiers invaded their convent armed with guns, sticks, and machetes. Their leader assured the sisters that they would not be harmed, but that they would be brought to Wamba, some fifty kilometers away, for their own protection. He told the sisters to gather whatever they needed to travel.

Sister Anuarite shakily threw some clothes and food into a bag, including a *pagne*, the all-purpose cloth that many African women wrap around their waist as a skirt, but also use for a variety of other purposes. Then she joined her sisters as they were loaded onto the truck: eighteen professed sisters, nine novices, and seven postulants. They could hear the raucous laughter and vulgar comments of the soldiers, who were planning to forcibly violate the sisters' vows of chastity. The sisters realized that the promise of safety had been false. They encouraged one another with glances and whispered prayers.

In her pocket, Sister Anuarite clutched the little statue of the Virgin Mary that she always kept there. Her other hand held her rosary, and she prayed for the courage to remain faithful to Jesus, no matter what happened.

Wherever they stopped, the soldiers drunkenly pillaged anything they could find. Finally, they stopped at the mission in Ibambi late at night. The priests of the mission had already been murdered. The soldiers smashed through the door of the rectory, then herded the sisters into one room where they were told to sleep on the floor. Sister Anuarite pulled out the old pagne she had packed and offered it to Sister Hélène to soften the ground for her head and shoulders. She gave the place she had found to sleep to another sister, finding a smaller space for herself. As the sisters tried to settle themselves to sleep, Sister Anuarite also tried to lighten the atmosphere. But all night long the soldiers harassed them with threats, insults, and vulgarity. Terrified, not one of the sisters closed her eyes.

Through the long night, Sister Anuarite's heart raced with anxiety. Would she be strong enough to give the ultimate witness to her Spouse if she was called upon to do so? Almost since she could remember, she had wanted to be a religious sister even though her mother and even some of the sisters had discouraged her. It was a decision that many of her own people couldn't understand.

Anuarite had been born November 29, 1939, the fourth of six girls. Her father, Badjudu, was a soldier who was often away from home, and Anuarite grew up cherishing his presence even though he was very strict. When she was four years old, her father's travels took him to the Holy Land. He was so impressed with the life of Jesus that he wrote to Anuarite's mother, Julienne, to advise her and the children to be instructed and baptized in the Catholic faith.

When Badjudu finally returned home, he decided that, since Julienne had given him no sons, he would take another wife. But Julienne, who was now Catholic, did not believe polygamy was right and separated from him. Anuarite never got over this separation, praying even on her profession day for her parents to be reunited.

At age nine, Anuarite started going to the mission school. She had to study harder than some of the other children if she wanted to pass. When she told her teacher—a sister—that she wanted to become a religious sister, her teacher responded that she couldn't be a sister with such low grades. When Anuarite told her mother that she wanted to enter the convent, her mother told her it was too soon.

Anuarite had to repeat a grade in order to qualify for secondary school, but with a great deal of hard work, she finally succeeded. Then, her mother gave her permission to enter the convent. She was fifteen years old—a typical age for young women to get married.

At first, Anuarite had found some aspects of convent life hard. She especially struggled with obedience and with being corrected for her faults. Gradually she realized that corrections could help her know herself better. And obedience was not about doing what the superior wanted but about doing *the will of God*—to whom she was consecrated. Anuarite's lively nature made her an excellent teacher and a joyful presence in the community. On August 5, 1959, Anuarite made her vows. Both her parents were present to celebrate with her, giving the community two goats as a gift.

She continued her studies, then returned to teach the upper primary classes. She was a beloved teacher who paid attention to the needs of the students who didn't fit in or who were known to be troublemakers. She gave herself so completely to her sisters and her duties that her health broke down, and she had to take time off to rest. But Anuarite loved her students so much that she couldn't stop at half-measures.

An extrovert, Anuarite was a warm and welcoming presence in her community. But she also could be too quick and abrupt in her speech. She struggled with her sharp impetuosity all her life but tried to make up by apologizing right away. The villagers and the sisters who lived with her would remember her most for her great generosity and kindness. With her favorite expression,

"Jesus alone," she gave voice to her deepest desire: to be faithful to Jesus in everything.

Now, in the darkness, Anuarite whispered in prayer. "O Jesus, give me the grace to die, even at this moment, rather than to abandon you."

The next day, the soldiers herded the sisters back onto the truck. As they approached a village near Wamba, they stopped. One of the Simba rebels, Chief Yuma Deo, ordered all of the sisters down from the truck, to be stripped of all religious articles. Their crucifixes were torn from around their necks. A rough hand grabbed Sister Anuarite's rosary. She clung to it, but it was wrenched away. The soldiers stamped on the pile of sacred objects, then tossed them into the forest. Then the men forced the sisters back onto the truck, which now took them to Isiro, another eighty kilometers away.

As Anuarite climbed back into the truck, she felt she would choke on the thick silence. Then spontaneously, the sisters started to pray the Rosary—and continued praying it throughout the rest of the trip.

When they arrived at Isiro, the sisters waited to be taken by van, group by group, to a house. One of the rebel soldiers, Colonel Ngalo, eyed Sister Anuarite. Becoming uncomfortable under his gaze, Sister Anuarite turned to the sister next to her, Sister Elizabeth Kahenga, and whispered, "I should run away."

Sister Elizabeth had also noticed the colonel's attention. She encouraged Sister Anuarite. "But you don't know this area, and it's nighttime. Ask Mother Leontine what to do."

Mother Leontine took Sister Anuarite by the arm, and together they climbed into the van for the second trip. "Don't worry," she told Sister Anuarite, "we'll go together." But one of the officers pulled Sister Anuarite out. Mother Leontine kept a firm grasp on her young sister's arm and followed her, insisting that they stay together. The two sisters were then brought by some soldiers to Colonel Ngalo's residence. He told Sister Anuarite bluntly, "You are to become my wife."

Mother Leontine immediately interposed, "This sister has made a vow of chastity; she is consecrated to God. You cannot take her as your wife."

Infuriated, the rebel Chief Deo slapped Mother Leontine in the face. "Do you dare refuse? I will call my soldiers, and we will assault all your sisters. Then I'll tie you up in a sack myself and throw you into the river." Mother Leontine did not give in. She refused to be separated from Sister Anuarite—even when Anuarite was forcibly taken to another room, she made sure the door was left open so she could hear her.

In the room, Colonel Ngalo repeated his demand. "You will be my wife, or I will kill you."

Heart pounding, Sister Anuarite stood silent but firm, refusing to even acknowledge his offer. Finally he added, "If you refuse, we'll kill your superior, too."

Shocked, Sister Anuarite finally answered with a plea. "Why would you kill her? Just kill me."

At this verbal proof of her resistance, Colonel Ngalo tore off her veil and started hitting her.

At the other house, the sisters were given rice and sardines. But they refused to eat until Sister Anuarite and Mother Leontine were returned to them. Colonel Olombe came to Ngalo's residence, bringing word that the sisters were refusing to eat. Ngalo asked Olombe to help him seduce Anuarite, and Olombe confidently agreed. He then reunited the two sisters with the other sisters so that they could eat together.

Sister Anuarite, bruised and shaken, tasted her food but couldn't eat. Inside, she was terrified. Would her fear betray her? When the other sisters comforted her, she simply said, "I am so troubled. Please pray for me. I am willing to die to preserve my vow of chastity but pray for me!"

After the meal, Colonel Olombe started to separate the sisters into different rooms, but the sisters refused to go, saying they would sleep in one room. Finally, the drunken Olombe agreed. He pulled Sister Anuarite and Sister Jean Baptiste outside and forced them into the van. As he stepped away, the two sisters jumped out of the van and tried to escape, but the Colonel caught them. Sister Anuarite told him, "I do not want to commit sin. If you want, kill me."

Crazed with rage, Olombe beat one sister then the other with his rifle butt. After he broke Sister Jean Baptiste's arm in three places, she fell unconscious. Despite her beating, Sister Anuarite remained upright on her knees. "I forgive you," she said, "because you do not know what you are doing."

He hit her repeatedly, but she made no sound. Finally, she murmured, "Just as I wanted," and collapsed to the ground. The two sisters lay unconscious for about fifteen minutes.

Some of the rebel soldiers who witnessed the ferocity of Colonel Olombe's drunken attacks on the sisters took his rifle, in case he decided to kill all the sisters, as he was loudly threatening to do.

Becoming more enraged because he couldn't find his rifle, Olombe called for more armed soldiers. Two more Simba rebels arrived, and he told them to stab Sister Anuarite in the chest. Each time, Sister Anuarite groaned softly with pain. Then Olombe shot her in the chest with a pistol.

Only then did he allow the sisters to take her tortured body into the house. She was barely breathing. One of the sisters cradled Sister Anuarite's head in her lap, calling her name. Without awakening, she died at about one o'clock in the morning.

Sure they would die soon, the sisters prepared themselves. They asked forgiveness of one another for any lack of charity, then started to sing the Magnificat, thanking God for the grace to follow in Sister Anuarite's footsteps. The singing unnerved the colonel, and he ordered them to stop. Finally, his drunken rage calmed.

The sisters were left the rest of that night at the mercy of the soldiers who threatened, hit, and kicked them. Only Sister Anuarite died that night, but the entire community underwent a true martyrdom.

Sisters in Christ, their sisterhood gave them the strength to resist the soldiers' harassment, threats, and beatings. Finally, in the morning, the sisters were allowed to leave. They asked for the body of Sister Anuarite, but the soldiers refused their request. Eight months later, her body was discovered in a common grave. A tiny statue of the Blessed Mother—who must have given Anuarite courage and strength in those last minutes—was found in her pocket.

Personal Challenge

What would be different if I were to reexamine my life through the eyes of Jesus and make radical choices in everyday situations to be a more loving and truthful person?

Prayer

Blessed Anuarite, radiant martyr of purity, pray for us! Drawn to the consecrated life at a young age, you shared a joyful life of prayer and service, as a sister among sisters. In the hours of crisis, your mutual faith and sisterly prayers strengthened you to once again offer your whole self to God, body and soul. Today, the world still cannot understand the choice for chastity and a radical fidelity to the Gospel. Protect us, as you protected your sisters in life and death, so that we, too, can offer our whole selves to God. Amen.

Facts About Her Life

~::~ Anuarite was not born into a Christian family but was baptized with her mother and sisters when she was about four years old.

~::~ Anuarite has many names:

> ✦ Her parents named her Nengapeta, a family name that refers to riches.
> ✦ She was baptized Alphonsine.
> ✦ When she started school, one of the sisters made a mistake and gave her the name of her sister, Anuarite, which means "one who laughs at war."
> ✦ At her profession of vows in the Sisters of the Holy Family, she was given the name Sister Marie-Clémentine.

~::~ Anuarite had a stammer that made it difficult for her to speak when angry or tense.

~::~ Anuarite was of average intelligence and struggled with school, taking more time to study and repeating at least one grade.

~::~ On her profession day, Sister Anuarite prayed that her parents would be reunited.

~::~ Anuarite is best remembered by the sisters with whom she lived for her great generosity and kindness, her cooking in the kitchen for feast days, and her lively ability to make the other sisters laugh.

~::~ Anuarite had a special love for the wayward girls in the school and gave them extra encouragement.

~::~ Her favorite saints were Saint Cecilia, Saint Agnes, and Saint Maria Goretti.

~::~ Sister Anuarite suffered from fragile health, especially migraine headaches.

~::~ Sister Anuarite's Marian devotion was nurtured by the well-loved book *The Glories of Mary*, written by her baptismal patron, Saint Alphonsus Liguori.

~::~ She kept a small notebook that included short prayers and personal reflections, recipes, dates, and her favorite passages from spiritual reading.

~::~ After the rebellion, having served several years in prison, Olombe showed up at the convent, asking for food. Mother Leontine gave him something to eat, saying, "Sister Anuarite forgave you; we must follow her example."

~::~ In 1985, at Sister Anuarite's beatification, her murderer asked the Pope to forgive him, and Pope Saint John Paul II publicly assured him of the Church's forgiveness.

In Her Own Words

"My resolution: To love the Lord because he has done great things for me; how great is his goodness!"

Reader's Guide for Blessed Marie-Clémentine Anuarite, page 192.

BLESSED ARE THE
PEACEMAKERS, FOR
THEY WILL BE CALLED
CHILDREN OF GOD.

Saint Elizabeth of Hungary

The Princess Who Found True Love

Born: 1207, Hungary

Died: November 16, 1231, at Marburg, Germany

Feast Day: November 17

Canonized: May 28, 1235, by Pope Gregory IX

Patron: brides, bakers, widows, Catholic charities, Franciscan Third Order

Elizabeth knew that, at first glance, they must not have looked like a royal couple. Sitting contentedly next to her, Ludwig was working his way through the most recent dispatch while she was stitching a blanket for her soon-to-arrive third child. She allowed her eyes to linger on her husband's strong hands, then impulsively reached over and intertwined her fingers with his. A smile broke his serious attention, and Elizabeth reveled in his tender glance. "My dark beauty," he murmured.

Elizabeth felt so blessed. She enjoyed every moment with her beloved Ludwig—whether she was sitting beside him in the great hall or they were riding together. She wore beautiful clothes because he enjoyed seeing her in them, although she wore a hair shirt underneath. When Ludwig was away and it was impossible for her to go with him, she dressed in mourning clothes until his return, when she would be the first to hurry out to meet him. For a while, she had worried that she loved her husband too much, but her confessor had assured her that her path to union with God was with and through her husband. She had finally realized this and had told him, "It is in God that I love my husband: may he who sanctified marriage grant eternal life."

Their love for each other was God's gift to carry them through the many challenges they faced, not just as a family with little Herman and Sophia, but also as the rulers of Thuringia (in those days the ruling couple were called the land-grave and the landgravine). Their responsibilities were heavy: rulers of a large territory, they were also obligated to serve the king of Germany, Frederick II.

Elizabeth reminisced happily as she stole another glance at her husband's handsome profile. She had first met Ludwig when she was only four years old. Her father, King Andrew of Hungary, had sent her to Wartburg Castle near Eisenach, Germany, to be raised with her betrothed, Landgrave Herman I's eldest son. She was accompanied by two ladies-in-waiting and a large dowry. It was a customary political arrangement, but as a four-year-old, she knew only that she was homesick and fearful. The boyish kindness of eleven-year-old Ludwig and his father had comforted her on her arrival, and then again two years later, when she had learned of her mother's murder.

As the little princess matured into a young woman, her friendship and respect for Ludwig grew. But she endured difficult times when Ludwig was away, especially after his father had died. With Hungary's power waning, his family no longer saw Elizabeth as a good match for Ludwig. They criticized her for her piety and her generosity to those who were less fortunate. When Ludwig became landgrave after his father's death, he publicly renewed his intentions to marry her. "I would more willingly part from a mountain of gold than from my betrothed!" he confided to a friend. Finally, when he was twenty-one and she fourteen (ages typical for a bride and groom at the time), he married her in a magnificent wedding—the church packed with royalty, knights, and ladies. Yet, it had not been too extravagant; Elizabeth had set aside a portion of the money intended for the wedding banquet to give to the poor.

What she remembered best from her wedding was his striking figure and the way his eyes lit up when he saw her approach the altar. But her Ludwig was much more than handsome. He was courageous and true, a chivalrous knight devoted to God and his people. He shared in her life of prayer, encouraged her in her many works of charity, and supported the decisions she made while he was away—even when she practically emptied their treasury to feed the families starving in the recent famine. Her husband helped her to build a hospital for lepers and didn't object that she herself nursed those who were in the hospitals and fed the hungry who came to the castle gates.

Now, as they sat together, Ludwig tried to get through all the messages quickly, so he could snatch a few undistracted minutes with his Bett. He knew his wife was still sometimes hurt by his family's criticism. Her lifestyle was a challenge to the aristocracy of their feudal world, even provocative at times. Many lords and ladies were generous, but Elizabeth gave of herself in the most

natural, direct, and complete way possible. Many of the aristocracy were too busy with politics, society, and their own lives to
stop to think of the suffering of the desperately poor people of
the land. His wife's generosity was her way of serving the people
and drawing closer to God. The more others criticized her, the
more he admired and loved her.

In addition, Ludwig knew that some of the court continued
to dislike Elizabeth, not only because she was Hungarian, but
also because she was so faithful to him. Such fidelity in courtly
circles was uncommon at the time partly because so many mar-
riages were prearranged. To the amazement of the sophisticated
court, Ludwig and Bett were a very happily married couple. Truly,
their union had been blessed by God! Until now . . .

Elizabeth suddenly noticed that Ludwig's frame had frozen.
He was reading intently, his brow furrowed.

"What is it, Ludwig?" she asked. "Another trip?" She recognized the seal of Frederick, who had now assumed the title of
emperor.

"Frederick is preparing for the next Crusade to keep his
promise to the Pope," Ludwig said. He turned to her; his eyes
filled with regret. "I won't be here for the birth of our next little
one," he said softly. "I am called to go with him."

To the Holy Land! Elizabeth felt her world crumble around
her. For a moment, blackness overshadowed her vision. The darkness cleared, and Ludwig's concerned face filled her eyes.

"Don't go, darling! It's too dangerous! You'll be away for at
least a year, maybe much longer! Please, for my sake, for the sake
of our child. Don't leave me now!"

Ludwig's face grew more troubled. "I have to go, Bett; it's my
duty to Frederick. God would not want me to neglect my duty."

"But your duty is also here, to your children, to your people. Even to me!" Elizabeth knew she wasn't being fair. Ludwig did have a duty to his king. But she couldn't let him go. Not so easily. Not when he might not come back.

"Let's pray about it," Ludwig urged. "I'm sure God will make my path clear."

Elizabeth felt sick with fear. She tried to listen in her prayer but instead found herself pleading with God to keep her husband safely by her side. Finally, worn out with her pleas and prayers, she spoke with Ludwig again. Ludwig was convinced that his going on Crusade was God's will for them. In the face of his conviction and her desire to do God's will, Elizabeth accepted his decision. "I will not hold you back. It is the will of God. I have given myself entirely to him, and now I must give you too!" Despite her pregnancy, she accompanied him on the first part of his journey. Their parting broke her heart, but Elizabeth choked back her tears. Her last glimpse of him was his upright figure saluting her as his horse pranced, eagerly leading the way. It was June 24, the feast of John the Baptist.

In the months that followed, Elizabeth anxiously awaited news of Ludwig while also preparing for the birth of their third child. Finally, in October, she gave birth to their second daughter, Gertrude. A few days later, the news arrived. On September 11, her husband had died in Otranto of a plague that had swept away many of the Crusaders.

Elizabeth was devastated. Unable to contain her grief, she shrieked out, "The world and all that gave me joy is dead to me!" After hours of uncontrollable sobbing, Elizabeth found her way to a large crucifix. Exhausted, she prayed simply, "You know, O Lord, that I loved him more than anything in this world because he loved you and because he was my husband. But you have taken him to yourself. I commend him and myself to your mercy. May your will be done in us."

She was a widow at twenty. Her five-year-old son, Herman, should inherit his father's title when he came of age. But Heinrich, Ludwig's brother and Herman's regent, assumed all authority as landgrave and banished Elizabeth from the castle in the middle of winter. He further ordered that no one was to give the family any aid, falsely accusing Elizabeth of squandering the family's wealth.

Driven out with nothing, Elizabeth took shelter that cold night in a pig shed, with her baby in her arms. Her faithful ladies-in-waiting joined her and, together with Elizabeth's children, they made their way to a nearby Franciscan monastery, where they asked the monks to sing a hymn of thanksgiving to God. Elizabeth wanted to thank God for the opportunity to experience some of the poverty and suffering he had endured on earth.

For some time, Elizabeth and her children were among the poorest of the poor. Daily she walked the streets, begging for scraps of food. Fortunately, news of what had happened reached her aunt, the abbess at Kitzingen, and she gave them shelter. Elizabeth's father and Ludwig's soldiers threatened Heinrich with severe action when they found out what he had done. Finally, when Ludwig's body was brought home to rest, Heinrich expressed his remorse to Elizabeth, who reconciled with him. The landgraviate and its title were returned to little Herman (although he never actually ruled; he died at age nineteen), and Elizabeth's properties were restored. She went to live at Marburg, where she established another hospital.

Elizabeth's uncle tried to pressure her into a new marriage. Emperor Frederick even inquired about her. But Elizabeth had made a sacred promise not to remarry and wanted to devote her life to the care of others, especially those who were poor and sick. A great admirer of her contemporary, Saint Francis, she had joined the Third Order of Saint Francis before her husband's death and now wore the Franciscan habit. Under the strict direction of her confessor, Father Conrad, she grew steadily in sanctity.

Worn out with her unceasing service, Elizabeth fell ill and died at the age of twenty-three. The cup of her short life had been very full: princess, wife of a powerful ruler, mother of three children, widow, and religious. She had suffered grief, calumny, loneliness, and betrayal, as well as the physical sufferings of hunger and penance. Yet to Elizabeth, only one thing had mattered: that the cup of her life overflow with love. In every circumstance, whether joyful or sorrowful, Elizabeth had responded with love—drawing ever closer to God, the true Love of her life.

Personal Challenge

In the spirit of Saint Elizabeth of Hungary, ask the Holy Spirit to show you any family relationships in which you could bring at least a little peace.

Prayer

Saint Elizabeth of Hungary, in your love for your husband and family, you lived God's will. As leader of your people, you didn't allow the luxuries surrounding you to distract you from responding to God's

call to serve him in those who are poor. Teach me how to live my voca-
tion to love. I pray that my family may grow in love and forgiveness
of each other. May I recognize God's call to serve others with the same
generosity and compassion you had. Help me to see the face of Christ
everywhere, especially in my family and in those who are suffering.
Amen.

Facts About Her Life

∾∷∾ Elizabeth's family includes several saints: her aunt was Saint
Hedwig, her daughter is Blessed Gertrude of Aldenberg, and
her great-niece, Saint Elizabeth of Portugal.

∾∷∾ Elizabeth's mother was murdered when Elizabeth was six
years old.

∾∷∾ Elizabeth and Ludwig encouraged each other on their journey to holiness. After his death, Ludwig was considered a
saint by his people. Although he was never canonized, he is
recognized as blessed.

∾∷∾ Ludwig would hold his wife's hand when she rose at night to
pray.

∾∷∾ We know so much about the details of Elizabeth's life because of the testimony of four servants, particularly her two
ladies-in-waiting, Isentrude and Jutta, who had been with
Elizabeth since her childhood.

∾∷∾ It is estimated that, while she was landgravine, Elizabeth
fed more than nine hundred people daily. She also provided
work, donating tools to men who needed them, and teaching
women how to spin.

~:~ Elizabeth was drawn to Franciscan spirituality and lifestyle and helped establish the Franciscans in Thuringia. Later, she would become the first Franciscan Tertiary in Thuringia (Franciscan Tertiaries are now known as Secular Franciscans).

~:~ After her husband's death and without his protection, Elizabeth fought to regain her property, not for herself, but so that her children would be provided for. She then gave her children to the care of those she trusted and dedicated herself to charitable service.

~:~ One form of penance that Elizabeth practiced was to refuse to eat any food that had been obtained unethically.

In Her Own Words

"How can I, a creature, wear a crown of gold when the Lord bears a crown of thorns and bears it for me?"

Reader's Guide for Saint Elizabeth, page 194.

Saint Catherine of Siena

Woman Afire

BORN: March 25, 1347, in Siena
DIED: April 29, 1380, in Rome
FEAST DAY: April 29
CANONIZED: 1461 by Pope Pius II
DECLARED DOCTOR OF THE CHURCH: 1970 by Pope Saint Paul VI
PATRON: Rome, Italy (with Saint Francis of Assisi), Europe, Dominican
  Tertiaries, nursing

The twenty-year-old mystic recluse Catherine Benincasa sat
stunned on the bench in her little room. What was she supposed to do? For three years, as soon as she had been allowed to
dedicate her life to God, she had devoted herself to a life of prayer
and contemplation while living at home with her family. She left
her bedroom—her "cell" as she liked to call it—only to go to
church and spoke to no one but her confessor. Jesus, who had first
appeared to her when she was six years old, had told her this was
a time of probation, a time to grow in self-knowledge and prepare

for Catherine's deepest desire—mystical union with him. And finally, just days ago, Jesus had espoused her to himself, giving her a ring she could see but which seemed invisible to everyone else.

This morning, she had begged Jesus to deepen her union with him, and he had hinted that he was sending her out into the world to do good to others. Now, his clear directive so surprised her that she didn't know what to think. Jesus had told her to go join her family for the midday meal!

Catherine hadn't eaten with her family for three years. She had been called to retreat from the world, and it had taken her family—especially her mother—several long years and painful conflicts to understand Catherine's desire for a life of solitude and prayer.

Catherine was the twenty-fourth of her parents' twenty-five children, many of whom died in childhood, including a twin sister who had died after birth. Her father was a dyer, and her mother the daughter of a poet. Catherine had been a lively but plain child. When she was only six years old, she had her first vision of Christ, and her childhood and adolescence were filled with visions and a deep life of piety.

When Catherine reached the marriageable age of twelve, family pressure, especially from her oldest sister Bonaventura, succeeded in getting her to dress up, even to color her hair to make herself more attractive. But Bonaventura died giving birth, and Catherine suddenly realized that she was no longer on the path to her true vocation. She asked the advice of a Dominican friar who was also a friend of the family. Initially he tried to persuade Catherine to obey her parents' wishes. But when she finally convinced him of her vocation, he had advised her to cut off her hair—a decisive gesture that would make her mother angry.

Finally, after some hesitation, Catherine did it to show her parents that she was serious.

But instead of giving in, her family decided that she needed firmer persuasion. To "help" her change her mind, they assigned Catherine to the tasks of the servants. Since she wanted solitude and silence above all, they even took away her bedroom. But the Lord had helped Catherine to find refuge within herself, to create an inner sacred space, so she could still speak to him and be at peace, even in the midst of the heavy chores.

Finally, Catherine had called her family together and explained that she had vowed her virginity to Christ and wanted to join the Dominican Tertiaries. Also known as the Mantellate, these were laywomen who shared in the Dominican spirituality and mission while living at home. Catherine's father, who had always been more understanding of his daughter's ways, joked that he could have a worse son-in-law. He and his wife gave her a room of her own and the peace to follow her vocation. Her mother even helped persuade the Dominican Tertiaries to allow Catherine to join them at the age of sixteen. Since joining them, Catherine had dedicated her life to prayer. It was not easy. She lived the ascetical practices of her times very strictly—going with barely any sleep, disciplining herself with chains and scourging, and eating only bread and water. Yet, Catherine had been very happy.

Now Catherine pondered these new words of Jesus which she found so unsettling. Was he sending her away? Had she done something wrong? All Catherine cared about was being with him! God knew how distracted she had been before she had "left" the world only a few years earlier. If she went back, she would not only be distracted and lose her sweet conversations with God. She would fall into sin!

Then, Jesus spoke again to reassure her. "Do not be afraid! I will not remove myself from you; rather, I want to draw you even closer to me through your charity for your neighbor."

Catherine had meditated on the words of the Gospel many times: *Whatever you do to others, you do to me.* Could she draw closer to her God through active charity? Still, she struggled with the idea of returning to an active life. She protested one more time. "But how can I, a woman, be useful to others? It is not fitting for women to teach and preach."

Jesus replied once more, "I pour out my grace where I will."

It was midday. Catherine suddenly realized that it didn't matter if she didn't understand. Doing God's will was most important, and what Jesus wanted was clear. So she got up from the wooden bench that also served as her bed, left her cell, and joined her family who were starting their meal. As she entered, all conversation fell away. In the surprised silence, her mother's eyes narrowed as she contemplated her youngest daughter, emaciated from fasting and penance, standing in the doorway. Then she nodded toward a place at the table and immediately started talking to one of Catherine's brothers. Catherine's father was pleased, welcoming his daughter back with a smile.

Catherine gradually reentered the swirl of life, but what she had feared did not come to pass. Instead, the world around her was transformed because she saw it in a new way—through God's eyes. She discovered a special joy in serving those who were least fortunate or despised by others—criminals, those who suffered from leprosy or in hospitals, and those who were troubled in mind and spirit. Catherine started to feel the force of the wisdom of the Dominican ideal: to communicate what one contemplates. And Jesus didn't disappear from her life. Instead, he seemed to delight in making his presence felt when she was out among the people—for example, causing her to fall into ecstasy while she was praying at church. The public signs from God earned deep respect from some, ridicule from others, and jealousy or hatred from still others. It also drew doubters, who, once they got to know Catherine, were likely to experience a profound conversion. Catherine was unperturbed by all this. She remained deeply humble, rooted in her real relationship with God and aware of her unworthiness. (When Catherine went into ecstasy after Communion and became unaware of her surroundings, some people who thought she was a fraud would actually throw her out of the church onto the street, beat her, and then abandon her there. Catherine never complained about this ill-treatment.)

As controversial a figure as Catherine initially was, she came to earn the trust and respect of many people of Siena and of some local Dominicans. A group of disciples gathered around her, and Catherine came to consider them her spiritual family. Catherine's charity, which had been initially focused on her family and the sick (including nursing victims of the plague that struck Siena), now seemed to shift toward teaching, advising, and spiritual guidance. She became known as a peacemaker, mediating family and territorial feuds. (At one point, Catherine supposedly kept three priests busy ministering to the people who had been converted in their encounter with her.) The general chapter of the Dominicans called Catherine to Florence in 1374, wanting to meet and probably also interrogate this young Dominican tertiary whose controversial reputation was spreading. Impressed by her responses to their questions, the Dominicans assigned Father Raymond of Capua as her confessor and spiritual director. He quickly became her friend, adviser, and follower. He also provided the trusted support of the Dominican Order for her important mission.

As Catherine grew more aware of the deep tears in the fabric of the unity of the Church and the harm that the discord was doing to the People of God, she became quite disturbed. Because politics and Church policy had become so deeply intertwined, the actions of Church officials were often politically driven and contrary to the Gospel. At the same time, many civil leaders sought to control the affairs of the Church using force and threats from the outside or corruption from within.

The feuds between the various regions of Italy grew more and more violent. While these touched Siena, Florence was in a particularly fierce struggle with the Papal States (areas under papal rule). Catherine's growing advocacy for peace and unity led her to begin a correspondence with Pope Gregory XI, who lived in Avignon, France. The Pope invited her to Avignon to mediate the feud between Florence and the Papal States. Catherine accepted, but she did not succeed in bringing peace at this time because the Florentine representatives were insincere. However, she met with Pope Gregory XI many times that summer and persuasively urged him to return the papacy to Rome. The papacy had been in Avignon for most of the fourteenth century and suffered from corruption, a loss of independence (it was subject to the threat of the French monarchy, as well as other French influences), and alienation from much of the Church in western Europe. Devout Christians everywhere wanted the Pope to return to Rome, to the See of Saint Peter and the place of the martyrdom of both Saints Peter and Paul, thus unifying the Church.

In her short time with the Pope, Catherine convinced him to return to Rome although he wavered when he faced the resistance of the mostly French cardinals. Finally, however, he left for Rome, and Catherine kept up her correspondence with him, encouraging him and pressing him to have the courage to do what was right. During this time, she again went to Florence to make peace. Violence broke out and attempts were made on her life, but Catherine did not flee. She actually regretted that she was not murdered, wanting to become a martyr for peace, until her spiritual director pointed out that her death could have been used as an excuse for more violence. Yet, Catherine finally succeeded in her mission for peace for the Florentines when Pope Gregory's successor, Urban VI, asked her once again to mediate.

Suffering from ill health and aware that her time on earth was coming to an end, Catherine returned to Siena and dictated her great spiritual work, *The Dialogue*. By this time, Catherine's friends would describe her as a "bag of bones." Yet, despite the great physical pain she must have always suffered, she remained lively and cheerful.

Pope Urban VI rapidly became very unpopular due to his harsh ways. Certain cardinals declared his election invalid and elected a new pope, setting him up in Avignon. Catherine had foreseen and predicted this great schism, but it broke her heart. Pope Urban VI called Catherine to Rome for desperately needed support. Despite her poor health, Catherine went to Rome and labored tirelessly for the unity of the Church. She received a vision of the Church as a great ship crushing her, and her fragile health really started to fail. After three months of intense suffering that she willingly offered for the unity of the Church, Catherine finally left this earth to enjoy the uninterrupted wedding banquet with her Spouse. It was April 29, 1380; Catherine was thirty-three years old.

Personal Challenge

When I am uncertain of what God is asking me to do, can I, like Saint Catherine of Siena, turn to prayer, trusting God to provide courage and direction?

Prayer

Saint Catherine of Siena, your vision of the world was transformed by your contemplation. And what you contemplated in your prayer, you shared with the world. You strove unceasingly for peace and for unity in the Church. Your relationship with the Church was both faith-filled and practical. You revered priests and bishops in their sacred office, and you both supported and challenged them to live up to their responsibilities. Today the Church still suffers: wounded, disillusioned, fractured by disunity. Ask Jesus to set me alight with the fire of his love. Guide me so that I can live the Gospel and become a voice for unity and peace in the midst of diversity. Amen.

Facts About Her Life

~::~ Catherine had her first vision of Christ when she was six or seven years old while walking home with her brother Stephen.

~::~ Catherine vowed her virginity to Christ when she was very young.

~::~ Catherine was very persuasive. In violent times when a feud could destroy a village or ravage a countryside, her tireless efforts to bring peace saved countless lives.

~::~ Catherine wrote 372 letters which we have today, as well as *The Dialogue,* and some prayers.

❧∷∼ Despite her visions, Catherine was quite practical. As a penance, she started to wear a hair shirt but replaced it with a chain she wore around her waist because she had discovered the hair shirt wasn't hygienic.

❧∷∼ Catherine was very intelligent but received no schooling. With effort, she taught herself to read the Liturgy of the Hours as a teenager. Much later, she learned to write. But she dictated most of her letters and *The Dialogue*.

❧∷∼ In 1375 in Pisa, Catherine received the stigmata, but she begged Jesus to keep it invisible. After her death, both the stigmata and her wedding band became visible.

❧∷∼ At the end of her life, Catherine felt that she was a failure for not being able to prevent or heal the schism caused by two men both claiming to be Pope.

❧∷∼ Catherine's holiness and influence in the affairs of her time have always been recognized, but recently the depths of her spirituality and mysticism have gained more attention.

❧∷∼ When he named her Doctor of the Church in 1970, Pope Saint Paul VI called her "Doctor of Unity."

In Her Own Words

"O Abyss! O eternal Godhead! O Sea profound! What more could You give me than Yourself?"

Reader's Guide for Saint Catherine, page 197.

BLESSED ARE THOSE
WHO ARE PERSECUTED
FOR RIGHTEOUSNESS' SAKE,
FOR THEIRS IS THE
KINGDOM OF HEAVEN.

Blessed Isidore Bakanja

Member of Mary's Family

Born: c. 1885 in the Belgian-controlled Congo, now the Democratic
Republic of Congo

Died: August 9 or 15, 1909

Feast Day: August 15

Beatified: April 25, 1994, by Pope Saint John Paul II

Patron: While he has not yet been declared a patron of particular causes
or groups, Isidore could be a patron of those who: suffer acts of
violence and racial hatred; live in Africa; need to forgive or to be
forgiven; suffer persecution for their faith in the workplace; wear the
scapular; want to unite their sufferings to the Passion of Jesus

I sidore Bakanja walked uneasily away from the house, fingering
the scapular he wore around his neck. His back was mostly
healed from the recent flogging by his boss, Andre Van Cauter,
the Belgian supervisor of the rubber plantation. He could hear
Van Cauter laughing and shouting drunkenly even though
Isidore had walked some distance away. Better to stay out of sight
for now, at least until he had decided what to do.

Isidore had known before he came that the bosses in this part of the Congo were not fond of Christianity. But he had never thought it would mean outright persecution for such a simple thing as wearing a scapular. He had also thought his previous boss, Reynders, a fair-minded employer, could protect him. But Reynders wasn't in charge here, and the plantation was run in a way that any decent Christian would have deplored. Although it was 1909, the European owners still treated the Congolese laborers as slaves. They could be beaten and harassed at the whim of the boss.

Why wearing his scapular and praying the Rosary were so abhorrent to the boss, Isidore wasn't sure, but it was clear that living his faith publicly was quickly becoming dangerous. Isidore suspected that Van Cauter's hostility to Christianity had something to do with its teaching that, in the eyes of God, all people were equal. His brothers and sisters might have to put up with being treated unfairly, but they didn't have to give away their dignity. In the sight of God, Isidore stood as an equal next to Van Cauter.

This was one reason Isidore was so proud of his newfound faith and eager to share it. The clash between European culture and the lifestyle and traditions of his Congolese people was turbulent and fraught with violence and oppression. The Church had an answer if only people would listen!

Isidore crouched on the ground. What was he going to do? Van Cauter's rule here was absolute. Isidore considered his options. He could go back to the heavy masonry he had been doing since childhood, but he wanted to improve himself, maybe even provide for a family someday. Being a domestic servant was much easier than masonry and offered opportunities for the future. And when he wasn't so tired at night, he could pray or talk to other people about Jesus.

Another option was to stop wearing his scapular and to pray in secret. But he didn't want to do that, either. One of Isidore's greatest joys was to share his newfound faith with others. Many people here were just like he had been a couple of years ago—they had not even heard about the loving God who sent his Son to save all God's beloved children. The other workers were curious about what he was doing when he knelt down to pray, and sometimes they asked him to tell them stories about this God who loved them. Although Isidore wasn't trained as a catechist, he had learned the stories well, and he loved to retell them, especially stories about Mary.

He remembered what the Trappist monks had told him before he received Baptism just three years ago. "When you wear the scapular, you are part of Mary's family." ("Scapular" translated to "Mary's habit" in Isidore's native language.) At his First Communion, he had promised himself that he would always wear the scapular.

But if he lived his faith openly, he might be beaten again. Or worse. Isidore had heard rumors about the violence at other plantations. But the hatred in Van Cauter's eyes and the way he expected Isidore to shrivel up in front of him didn't just make Isidore afraid. It also stirred up something deep in Isidore's soul. He straightened with decision. He would *not* deny God, nor his own dignity and manhood. He was a child of God! It would be dangerous, but he would stand up to this oppressive boss on behalf of all his people, affirming their human rights, even the right to practice their faith.

As Isidore walked back toward the house, he found himself on alert but at peace with what he had decided to do. *Mary will protect me*, he thought. *I don't need to be afraid, no matter what happens.*

Isidore went back to his duties and prudently stayed out of Van Cauter's sight. But he soon heard Van Cauter calling his name from out in the yard. A feeling of foreboding clutched at Isidore's gut, but he walked out of the house toward his employer.

"Yes, boss!" he said, expecting a vitriolic verbal attack.

"Take off that thing!" growled Van Cauter in a drunken voice, gesturing at Isidore's chest.

Isidore said nothing, simply stood straight and tall. His heart was beating rapidly. This was the showdown he had been dreading. "Holy Mary, Mother of God, pray for me!" he prayed silently.

Van Cauter's rage erupted. He attacked Isidore, ripped at his shirt and tore off the scapular, knocking him to the ground. Shocked, Isidore lay there for a moment. Before he could rise, a blinding series of blows exploded on the side of his head and his neck, stunning him. He tried to curl up to protect his head but couldn't.

"You there, get the whip!" Van Cauter shouted to the other domestic servants watching. One of them ran to get it and held it out to Van Cauter. "Keep it!" Van Cauter shoved it back. "Whip him with all you've got!"

Isidore opened his eyes and tried to focus. He had worked side by side with these men—his countrymen. Then he saw the whip made from animal hide—with nails firmly fixed at the ends. Isidore feebly tried to get up. Van Cauter savagely kicked him in the face. "You two, hold him face down. Now!" he screamed at the laborers. "Or I'll beat you in his place!"

One frightened man stood over Isidore and started whipping. The pain ripped through Isidore's back, the nails tearing deep furrows on his back. Isidore kept silent at first, but then the nails struck through to the bone. Overwhelmed by the pain, Isidore screamed.

The young man stopped whipping him, perhaps frightened by the blood or the screams. The other two let him go. Isidore was too weak to do anything but try to roll over onto his side. "My God!" Isidore cried. He begged Van Cauter for mercy. "You're killing me!"

But Van Cauter, blinded by rage, kicked Isidore all over his head and neck. Then he ordered another laborer to continue whipping. The laborers lost count. Over 250 times, the nails ripped through Isidore's body. He endured the excruciating pain long past what he thought humanly possible. His shrieks dwindled to whimpers as he simply struggled to keep breathing. Finally, the laborers were too exhausted to continue. Van Cauter ordered them to drag Isidore into a hut of the plant, where Van Cauter chained his legs together so that Isidore couldn't even relieve himself and abandoned him to his agony.

Sometime later, Van Cauter unchained Isidore and dragged him out to the bush, ordering him to walk to the next village. An inspector named Dorpinhaus was coming to inspect the plantation. He had a reputation for fairness, and Van Cauter didn't want any trouble. But Isidore wasn't able to walk; his back was one open wound. He hid in the bush until he saw the inspector nearby. Then, supporting himself with two sticks, Isidore managed to drag himself toward the inspector. When Dorpinhaus saw Isidore's condition, he was horrified. He had his staff bring Isidore by boat to a nearby plantation. But infection set in, and despite the care he received, it was soon clear Isidore would not recover. Isidore asked his caregivers to send a message to his mother, any priest they could find, and perhaps a judge. "Tell them I have been attacked because I am a Christian."

Isidore tried to unite his sufferings with Jesus in his Passion, especially with his scourging. Two missionaries heard about what happened and visited him. After he told them his story, they gave him the sacraments and encouraged him to forgive Van Cauter. "I already have," he told them. "If I die, I'll pray for him in heaven."

Isidore suffered in agony from his wounds and infection for six months. Finally, he succumbed to septicemia. It's unknown exactly how old Isidore was when he died, but he was probably in his early twenties. Friends testified to his humble industriousness and to his joy in sharing his faith with others. Isidore Bakanja was buried as he had lived and died, with his scapular around his neck and his rosary in his hand.

Personal Challenge

What is one way that I, like Blessed Isidore Bakanja, can be truer to the person God calls me to be as a baptized Catholic, even when it calls for great heroism?

Prayer

Blessed Isidore Bakanja, you grew up in the midst of injustice and oppression. Discovering the history of God's love for us, especially in sending us his Son Jesus, transformed your whole life. You stood up to oppression with courage and dignity. You refused to betray your faith, your relationship with God, your very identity, even when it cost you your life. And when you were dying, you forgave the man who murdered you. Help me to treasure the grace of my Baptism. In these times troubled by prejudice, terrorism, and oppression, free me from bitterness so that I can forgive those who are blinded by hatred. Help me to stand up for the dignity of every human person and unite all my sufferings to Jesus' Passion and Death, sharing with you in the hope of his glorious Resurrection. Amen.

Facts About His Life

~:~ In 1904, Bakanja left his home village and was employed as a stone mason by the government, where he met a Christian for the first time: his foreman, Linganga, a recent convert.

~:~ Bakanja received instruction from the Trappist monks, who encouraged great devotion to Mary, including wearing the scapular and praying the Rosary.

~:~ Bakanja was baptized with the name "Isidore" on May 6, 1906. He was between seventeen and twenty-two years old. His baptismal certificate is the first written document we have about him.

~:~ The simple way he lived and witnessed to his faith attracted friends and those he met to the Christian faith.

~:~ Isidore had been a Christian for about three years when he was brutally beaten and died for witnessing to his faith.

~:~ After Isidore Bakanja's death, Andre Van Cauter was arrested and spent several years in jail.

~:~ Isidore is often listed as a "catechist and martyr," but he received no training as a catechist. His joy prompted him to share his faith with others.

~:~ The process for Isidore's beatification was delayed almost immediately because the Belgian government didn't want negative publicity about its conduct toward Isidore Bakanja, the Church, or the Congolese people.

~:~ In 1976, a group of lay catechists in Zaire (now the Democratic Republic of Congo) raised the possibility of Isidore Bakanja's beatification.

In His Own Words

When dying, he said that he forgave his persecutor, and even more: "If I die, I'll pray for him in heaven."

Reader's Guide for Blessed Isidore, page 199.

Saint Mary MacKillop
(Mother Mary of the Cross)
A Bit of Heaven

BORN: January 15, 1842, in Fitzroy, Victoria, Australia
DIED: August 8, 1909, in North Sydney, New South Wales, Australia
FEAST DAY: August 8
CANONIZED: October 17, 2010, by Pope Benedict XVI
PATRON: Australia, abuse victims

"But, Mother, what shall we do? You have certainly heard the rumors about the priest. It is said that he is abusing children."

"*It is said. . . . There are rumors. . . .* We must be careful, sisters. Remember, he is a priest of God."

"Yes, but Mother, the children are *our* main concern."

"You are certainly correct, Sister. The children are foremost. I will go to Father Woods. He will know how we should proceed."

Mother Mary of the Cross went directly to speak with Father Julian Woods, her confidante and cofounder of the Sisters of Saint Joseph of the Sacred Heart. He received her immediately.

"Thank you, Sister Mary, for coming to me. I will inform Bishop Sheil and leave the matter in his hands."

Bishop Laurence Sheil of Adelaide, Australia, took action, and after an investigation had the accused priest sent back to his home diocese in Ireland. However, a backlash would certainly be felt. The priest in question had many friends, and they were determined to make the whistle-blowers pay. As it was, some persons resented Father Woods, who held the office of director of Catholic schools in the diocese, for his strict management of the schools. How better to impress on him their indignation at his intervention than to strike out at his Josephites?

Although he had done the right thing by banishing the abusive priest from Australia, Bishop Sheil now had to endure the wrath of that priest's friends. *Something must be done*, he thought. *I can't deal with all this dissension and keep the diocese running smoothly.*

When Mother Mary received notice of the bishop's summons, she discussed it with one of her sisters. "Well, His Excellency is requesting my presence at once. He says there is an urgent matter to discuss."

"Do you suppose it is in reference to the exile of the priest?" the sister suggested.

"Oh, no, that matter is closed. I am sure His Excellency wants to discuss something to do with our various schools. I will set out in the morning."

Any preoccupations Mother Mary might have had were allayed by the cordial welcome she received at the bishop's residence.

"Please, Mother, have a seat. Let me get right to the matter at hand. I would like to see some minor changes in the Josephite rule . . ."

Immediately uncomfortable, Mother MacKillop sat forward as if to object.

"Mother, please, hear me out. It has come to my attention that difficulties have arisen from your handling of finances. Most of the schools are in considerable debt . . . and disrepair, I might add. And do sit back, Mother. Listen carefully to me. The priests in a number of locations are asking me to intervene in this matter. To assist you, Mother."

"But, Bishop Sheil, I have Father Woods, a very competent man. Why, you yourself have appointed him to various posts of responsibility in the diocese. I'm sure he . . ."

"Mother, Mother! We both know that Father Woods is a fine man, competent in many areas, but we all know he is somewhat of a visionary, an idea man. I've also heard that he allows a pseudo-mysticism to grow among the sisters. It is common knowledge that you are the true founder and former of the Sisters of Saint Joseph, and this is why I have called you here, not Father Woods."

"Your Grace, I cannot agree to anything without the approval of Father Woods. We have done this work together."

"You need not consult him, Mother. You will only need to inform him of what I am telling you. As of today, I am assuming direction of the finances of the Josephites and of all their schools and institutions."

"But, Your Grace, you know we mainly serve the poorest students who come from the poorest families. Certainly, it is clear that little money is available in most of our schools. We have chosen to serve the poor, the neediest of God's people."

"And I am sure, Mother, that it is clear to you that I have made a decision. From now on everything will go through me."

"With utmost respect, Your Excellency, I must insist that things remain in our hands. God has entrusted this work . . ."

"The diocese and its institutions are my responsibility, Mother Mary, and I will be obeyed. You are dismissed. I will expect your letter of compliance."

In dismay Mother MacKillop returned to the sisters' home. She considered and reconsidered the bishop's demand but could not reconcile his words with what she knew God was asking of her. So she did the only thing she could do, and that was delay. She simply put her trust in Divine Providence.

Soon enough, however, she received not a letter, but a visit from the bishop himself, with several priests. "Call the community together, Sister Mary," the bishop demanded. When the sisters had assembled, the bishop directed Sister Mary to kneel before him. As everyone looked on in dumbfounded silence, Bishop Sheil pronounced the terrifying words. "Because of your disobedience and spirit of rebellion, I excommunicate you from the Church. You are to have nothing to do with the Sisters of Saint Joseph. You are no longer a member of this institute but are to return to the world simply as Mary MacKillop."

How can this be? she prayed. *My good Lord, how can this happen?* However, in obedience Mary quietly stood up and left the convent. She took up residence with a Presbyterian family with whom she had been friends. Because of this sad event, many of the Sisters of Saint Joseph of the Sacred Heart opted to be reformed into diocesan communities rather than be forced to give up their vocations altogether.

While Mary continued to pray and suffer her fate silently, several other priests were petitioning Rome on her behalf. Meanwhile, God was unfolding his own plan. Bishop Sheil became ill and was not expected to recover. That led him to rethink what he had done, and he lifted the excommunication of Mary MacKillop. Joyfully she was reunited with her sisters. She did not hold a grudge against anyone involved in her suffering, and neither would she allow any of the sisters to speak badly of the bishop or of the priests who had conspired against her. "I feel only a very great love for those who persecuted us," she admitted. Sister Mary did not take her religious name lightly. She was Sister Mary *of the Cross*, and to her this meant she would willingly accept whatever came to her as a share in the saving action of Christ.

Sister Mary busied herself with the work of God. She visited the various schools, hospitals, and homes she had founded. She wrote constantly to the sisters, encouraging them to be prayerful and generous in whatever work they were doing for God's people. She was a person of great hopefulness and perseverance, as well as a gracious and kindly woman. She always had an excuse ready for those who offended her and a loving motivation for those who exhibited personal failures. It wasn't that Sister Mary was blind or unobservant of those around her, but she preferred to always show the love of God. Once she admitted, "Yes, at present I do have some enemies. God has allowed this. But, they are beloved enemies whom I am sure would rather be my friends if they could only see how things really are."

In the years that followed her great trial, Mary was elected as superior general of her institute. She travelled extensively throughout Australia and New Zealand, beginning many schools and other charitable works. In 1873 Mother Mary MacKillop traveled to Rome to ask for papal approval for the Sisters of Saint Joseph. Pope Pius IX appreciated all she had accomplished and gave his blessing. The constitutions of the congregation were slightly modified regarding poverty, and full authority was placed in the hands of the superior general.

Many young women asked admittance to the Josephites, and everything seemed to be moving ahead. However, in 1885 a new conflict arose. The bishops of Australia decided that despite Rome's approval of the new institute and its rules, the religious in their dioceses must be under the direct control of the diocesan bishop, and not of a superior general. Once more Mother Mary MacKillop was removed from any position of governance. After another few stressful years, Rome again set things straight. However, by this time a new superior general had taken office. Mother Mary became her willing and valued assistant. They made great strides in meeting the needs of the Australian people, especially regarding the education of children. No sacrifice was too much for Mary or her beloved sisters.

Over the years, Mother Mary began to have health problems, first with crippling rheumatism and then with a series of strokes that left her hands impaired. Despite these infirmities she was again elected superior general, and she continued in that position until her death in August 1909. As long as she could manage to do so, Mother Mary wrote encouraging letters to her sisters. "Let our life together be like a bit of heaven on earth. No matter what swirls around outside, no matter the humiliations and sufferings, among us there should be only love and charity."

Personal Challenge

When others stand in the way of what God is asking me to do, can I meet these sufferings and difficulties with the same integrity and courage that Mother Mary MacKillop showed?

Prayer

Saint Mary of the Cross, you were a woman of great fortitude and heroic charity. A true daughter of the Cross, you willingly bore humiliations and endured injustice in order to accomplish God's will. You were well aware of the strength that accompanies righteousness and of the graces that flow from persecution. Now in blessedness, continue your care for all those who suffer abuse. Help them turn to the Lord for help and lift up their hearts in love. Amen.

Facts About Her Life

- ~::~ She was born Mary Helen MacKillop, the eldest of eight children of Scottish immigrants to Australia.

- ~::~ Her family was poor and survived mainly on the wages made by the children.

- ~::~ Well-educated by her father, Mary began work as a governess at age fourteen.

- ~::~ She met Father Julian Tenison Woods at Portland, Victoria, where she opened a boarding school for girls in 1864.

- ~::~ With two of her sisters, she joined Father Woods to open a free Catholic school in Penola, South Australia, in 1866.

~:~ In 1867 with Father Woods, she founded the Sisters of Saint Joseph of the Sacred Heart, the first religious order native to Australia.

~:~ By 1871, 130 sisters were working in forty schools and other works of charity throughout South Australia and Queensland.

~:~ Mother Mary was buried at Gore Hill in North Sydney.

~:~ Due to popular devotion, her remains were transferred to a memorial chapel in Sydney in 1914.

~:~ In 2009, the cure of Kathleen Evans of lung and brain cancer in the 1990s was recognized as a second miracle attributed to Mother Mary's intercession, leading to her canonization.

~:~ She is the first Australian canonized saint.

~:~ When she was canonized, there were 1,200 Sisters of Saint Joseph of the Sacred Heart.

~:~ In 1985, Australian rose growers developed the Mary Mac-Killop rose.

~:~ Several films and stage productions have depicted her life.

In Her Own Words

"See how God has protected his work and brought good out of all our crosses. Thus he will ever do if we but put our *trust* in him and humbly distrust ourselves."

Reader's Guide for Saint Mary MacKillop, page 202.

Reader's Guides

Saint Francis of Assisi

Blessed are the poor in spirit, for theirs is the kingdom of heaven (Matthew 5:3).

Francis was like the rich young man Jesus spoke to in the Gospel (Mt 19:16–30), but Francis overcame his sadness, gave everything away, and wholeheartedly embraced a life of radical poverty. The irrepressible joy that shone from his poverty of spirit drew many to the imitation of Christ.

Discussion Questions

~:~ One of the most iconic episodes in the young Francis' life takes place before the bishop when he stripped himself of his clothes and returned them to his father. From then on, Francis had to rely completely on the providence of God, having nothing to call his own. How did you think of "poverty of spirit" before reading the life of Saint Francis? How does learning about this saint's life change the way you understand your desire within your own vocation to have a free heart and an uncluttered life?

~:~ Francis was used to being the carefree merrymaker, the life of every party. After he returned from his second military adventure, he yearned for something deeper, more real—but what? Does the inner wrestling of Francis resonate with you? What is most helpful about his experience in recognizing your own spiritual emptiness and the call of God for something "more"? After reading Saint Francis' story, what about his life attracts you?

~:~ Faith in God has consequences for our whole life. It means living with thanksgiving, respecting the dignity of all people, using material goods in such a way that they bring us closer to God, and trusting God in every circumstance. Which of these characteristics of a disciple's life is easiest for you? Which is the most challenging? What are the most enlightening and encouraging parts of Saint Francis' story for you as you renew your own following of Jesus?

~:~ Which of the characters in the story—Francis, Pietro his father, or Pica his mother—do you relate to most? How could each of them live their vocation and responsibilities with poverty of spirit? Talk about the challenges of each and how they are reflected in the experience of people in your life.

Read ~:~ Reflect ~:~ Respond

~:~ The Beatitudes "depict the countenance of Jesus Christ and portray his charity . . . ; they shed light on the actions and attitudes characteristic of the Christian life" (CCC

1717). Quietly reflect on these passages of Scripture and the *Catechism*, opening your heart to the way the first beatitude might be inviting you to follow Jesus more closely: Matthew 6:26–30, Mark 10:17–31, Deuteronomy 15:11, Psalm 41:1–3, and *Catechism of the Catholic Church* 2544–2550.

~::~ To live the Beatitudes in our life is to discover the joy of bringing peace to the world. Pray with these passages of Scripture and the *Catechism* and ask Jesus to show you how he is calling you to be his hands and his feet in the world: Psalm 116, Luke 19:1–10, Philippians 3:9–11, and *Catechism of the Catholic Church* 222–227, 2447–2448.

Saint Juan Diego

Blessed are the poor in spirit, for theirs is the kingdom of heaven (Matthew 5:3).

A simple, uneducated man, but wise and willing, Juan Diego took the evangelization of his people squarely on his shoulders when he accepted Mary's commission.

Discussion Questions

~:~ Juan Diego spoke to our Lady with a familiarity not often seen even among the saints. Have you ever experienced Mary's solicitude and powerful intercession in your life? Has it made a difference in the way you speak with her and call upon her when you need her intercession for a special need? What qualities of Juan Diego's trust in his Lady are most attractive to you?

~:~ Juan Diego described himself as a tail-end, a leaf, the bottom of the pile. He showed a remarkable simplicity and a willingness to serve, carrying out a mission for which he clearly felt he was not prepared. Have you ever felt like Juan Diego? What in this story could be helpful for you to live this deep poverty of spirit in great confidence and trust?

~:~ Has this story changed your understanding of what it is to be "poor in spirit"? What about Juan Diego's humility and trust in God draws you? What doesn't make sense to you? Have you already seen the power of humble trust in your own life or in the life of another? What did that look like?

~:~ Reflect on Mary's solicitude for Juan Diego. She said to him: "Am I not your Mother? Aren't you beneath my shadow, protected by me? Aren't you within the folds of my mantle and within the embrace of my arms? Is there anything that you need?" How did you consider devotion to Mary before reading this story? What was most illuminating about Marian devotion in the appearance of Our Lady of Guadalupe to Juan Diego? How might you turn to Mary, trusting in her protection, embraced by her arms?

Read ~:~ Reflect ~:~ Respond

~:~ Mary, the Immaculate Virgin and Mother of God, continues in heaven to exercise her maternal role, intercedes for all the members of Christ, and shines forth as a sign of certain hope. Deepen your relationship with Mary, the mother of Jesus and your mother, using these passages: Luke 1:39–56; John 2:1–12; Acts 1:12–14, 2:1–4; and *Catechism of the Catholic Church* 967–971, 975.

~:~ In a world where wealth, notoriety, status, and fame are considered the path to happiness, embracing the values of the Beatitudes in our everyday choices leads us to find our ultimate joy in God who is the source of every good. As you reflect on these passages, ask the Spirit to deepen your desire for this joy: Proverbs 11:2, Isaiah 40:31, Micah 6:8, Luke 14:11, James 4:10, and *Catechism of the Catholic Church* 1723, 2556–2557.

Saint Germaine Cousin

Blessed are those who mourn, for they will be comforted (Matthew 5:4).

A young French shepherdess whose life was afflicted by sickness and neglect, Germaine achieved a high degree of virtue and mystical prayer.

Discussion Questions

~:~ In Germaine's story, the beatitude that those who mourn are blessed, fortunate, and will be comforted characterizes the life not only of Germaine, but also that of her mother and father. Mourning, in the beatitude, has multiple meanings. It certainly refers to mourning over the loss of loved ones. It also opens a new perspective on mourning over the loss of hopes and dreams, mourning over one's own sin or the sin of others, and feeling grief over weakness and sin that leads to conversion of hearts and a transformed life. Explore the multiple ways in which Germaine and her parents "mourned." Explore a time when you "mourned" in one of these ways.

~:~ How have you experienced the spirit of God's comfort in your difficulties?

~:~ What were the most difficult aspects of Germaine's situation for you? What is your response to her spirit of trust in God amid her suffering? Do you think it is possible to translate into your own life Germaine's trust in God and courageous strength to stand for what is right?

~::~ Tell the story of a situation in which God turned the most unlikely of events into an encounter of grace for you. In what way did this make a difference in your life? In your relationship with God?

Read ~::~ Reflect ~::~ Respond

~::~ Germaine's experience of suffering at the hands of her stepmother marked her entire life. She made profound and courageous choices to continue to love and to forgive, and her trust in God only grew stronger. Reflect on your response to difficult situations in your own life through these passages: Isaiah 49:15, 64:7; Hosea 11:1; Luke 14:10; 1 John 1:29–31; and *Catechism of the Catholic Church* 1721, 2222–2223.

~::~ When times are tough, it is difficult to trust that God sees and hears us, that he is with us, and that he cares about what happens to us. As you remember one of these difficult times in your own life, pray with these psalms: Psalm 25:4–5, 37:4, and 91:14–16.

Saint Monica

Blessed are those who mourn, for they will be comforted (Matthew 5:4).

Saint Monica is the patron of wives and mothers because she lived her whole life in the hope of bettering strained relationships and winning for God the hearts of those she loved. Her efforts and tears were rewarded with the conversion of both her husband and her son.

Discussion Questions

~:~ Monica's life was overflowing with suffering and tears but also, after Augustine's Baptism, with gratitude and peace. In this story, with which feelings do you most resonate? After reading her story, what would you consider her secret in not becoming overwhelmed with emotion in both difficult and positive situations?

~:~ Have you experienced for yourself Monica's love for a child who has left the practice of the Faith? What is most illuminating about her example for you? What is most challenging?

~:~ Sometimes, struggles of life and times of mourning seem to stretch over long periods and make sense only through the perspective of the whole arc of our life or that of others. In what way has Monica and Augustine's story illuminated your journey? What in particular has given you hope?

~:~ Monica suffered in a marriage that was very difficult. When her husband died, she pursued her son Augustine who had rejected the faith. She turned to priests and bishops for consolation and advice. Even though she felt alone in her life-mission for the salvation of her family, she did have connections to others in whom she shared courage and comfort. Tell your own story of how deep connections with others have been a way of giving and receiving wisdom and encouragement.

Read ~::~ Reflect ~::~ Respond

~::~ The life of Monica shows us that when we mourn for what we have lost and for the brokenness of humanity, we can turn to God with trust knowing that he does not wish for any to perish. Reflect on your own times of mourning as you pray with these passages: Matthew 18:14, Ephesians 1:3–11, 1 Timothy 2:3–4, Hebrews 10:10, and *Catechism of the Catholic Church* 2822–2825.

~::~ If our prayer is persevering and united with the prayer of Jesus, we can have the trust and boldness of children that we will obtain all that we ask in his name. Let these passages strengthen your heart to persevere in doing good: Luke 18:1–8, Galatians 6:9, Philippians 1:6, Colossians 4:2–6, and *Catechism of the Catholic Church* 2736–2742.

Saint Bernadette

Blessed are the meek, for they will inherit the earth (Matthew 5:5).

A sickly, illiterate child of an insignificant family is visited by the Blessed Virgin and entrusted with a message of penitence and prayer. Her docility and humility lead to the establishment of one of the greatest healing shrines in the world: Lourdes.

Discussion Questions

~:~ As soon as word got around that Bernadette had seen a Lady in the cave at Massabielle, she was quickly thrust into a series of circumstances that she couldn't control. Have you been in a similar situation? What has been your response? A meek person makes a deliberate choice to believe in God's ability to guide events and to see the larger vision of what God is bringing about. What was most illuminating to you about the way Bernadette handled all the pressure she was under throughout her life?

~:~ The Immaculate Conception is the Church's teaching that Mary, from the moment of her conception, was preserved from original sin by a singular grace, a privilege of God given to her in view of the merits of her son Jesus who has redeemed the world. After reading the story of Bernadette, how do you understand the way Mary cares for her children? Are you devoted to the Blessed Virgin under a specific title?

~:~ Saint Bernadette was born into very difficult circumstances, personally bearing throughout her life the consequences of living in poverty. Her patient endurance
was a mark of her meekness throughout the stages of her
life, demonstrating her inward resilience in a position of
weakness. Share a time when God's grace made it possible for you to live through difficult circumstances with
an inner strength and resilience.

~:~ Bernadette was considered to be so unextraordinary that
as a child, and later as a sister in Nevers, she was treated
very poorly. What are some important lessons we can
learn from the way Bernadette let go of the need to be
recognized as a visionary while at the same time deter-
minedly carrying out the mission Mary had given her?

Read ~:~ Reflect ~:~ Respond

~:~ If we are growing in meekness like Saint Bernadette, we
are pursuing virtue and acting consistently with integrity in the situations of our everyday life. As you reflect
on these passages, let them shed light on your own daily
choices: Psalm 25:9, 37:11; Matthew 5:5; 1 Peter 2:20–
23; James 3:13; and Catechism of the Catholic Church
1803–1811.

~:~ Mary is "full of grace," redeemed from the moment of her
conception by virtue of the merits of Jesus Christ and
preserved free from all stain of original sin. Learn more
about Mary's divine motherhood: Luke 1:26–38; John
2:1–10, 19:26–27; Revelation 12; and Catechism of the
Catholic Church 490–495, 502–507.

Saint Gregory the Great

Blessed are the meek, for they will inherit the earth (Matthew 5:5).

Although he wished to decline his appointment to the papacy, Gregory accepted and placed himself and his talents so wholeheartedly at the service of the Church as to be truly deserving of the title "the Great."

Discussion Questions

~::~ Gregory was Christlike in meekness and a fearless shepherd of the Church. Characteristics of a meek leader are humility, patience, a servant-like attitude, as well as courage and power united with kindness and trust in God and his care for us. How did you understand meekness before reading this story? How do you understand it now?

~::~ Have you ever encountered a situation where you struggled between, on the one hand, following what you wanted to do, or what you felt God had shown you was your mission in life, and, on the other hand, taking up something new that was clearly being asked of you and was something that was desperately needed? After reading the life of Saint Gregory, how would you live through this situation differently in the future and allow God's love for you to shape your life?

~::~ Meek leaders are self-aware. They know their weaknesses and their blind spots but don't use this as an excuse for passivity and withdrawal. Instead of jostling for power and position, they are prophetic people who forget about themselves for the sake of serving others. How might you respond to situations that call for courage and boldness?

~::~ Describe a time when you were asked to take on a project or were thrown into a situation you hadn't expected and for which you weren't prepared. What were your fears? In what way did you surprise yourself or others? What were the temptations to vanity and arrogance? In what way will Gregory's example guide you through these types of situations in the future?

Read ~::~ Reflect ~::~ Respond

~::~ In the Church, the consecrated life is a way of following Christ more closely so that by imitating the Lord's self-emptying, one can more fully be a sign of God's presence to the world. Read these passages to learn more about the religious life: Matthew 4:18–22, 16:24, 17:1–9; John 12:1–8; and *Catechism of the Catholic Church* 925–927, 931–933.

~::~ Christ still shepherds the People of God and increases its numbers through a variety of offices and ministries instituted for the good of the whole Body of Christ. As you read the following passages, ask the Lord for a growing appreciation for those who shepherd the flock of God: Matthew 16:18–19; Acts 20:28; Ephesians 4:11; 1 Peter 5:1–4; and *Catechism of the Catholic Church* 871–879.

Saint Pier Giorgio Frassati

Blessed are those who hunger and thirst for righteousness, for they will be filled (Matthew 5:6).

Pier Giorgio Frassati was a young man who, in his short twenty-four years of life, reached a maturity of virtue and grace that was beautifully manifested in his exuberance for life and his generous spirit of hidden service.

Discussion Questions

~::~ The urgency that Jesus speaks of in the beatitude that those who hunger and thirst for righteousness will be satisfied is often lost on us. Where we live, food and water are probably plentiful. But in Jesus' time, and in many parts of the world today, many go hungry, and water is scarce. To hunger and thirst, therefore, means to pursue holiness with energy, urgency, and the determination of someone who is starving for Christ and who strives to live in a Christlike way. How do you understand the call to holiness after reading the story of Pier Giorgio? What impresses you most about his holiness?

~::~ What are the most difficult or challenging points in Pier Giorgio's story for you personally? What are the most encouraging?

~::~ Do you think of the purpose of your life as becoming one with Jesus Christ and serving others by showing his love to them? Share the story of some incident in your life where you were consciously aware of your call to holiness. What helped you in the moment to remember the deep meaning of your life?

~:~ Pier Giorgio climbed the mountain of holiness with his many steps to the homes of the poor. He was known as someone who prayed and was serious about his journey of faith. At the same time, he was nicknamed "Terror," and was filled with joy. Describe a time when you experienced these characteristics of Pier Giorgio's holiness in your own life. What was that like? What makes it challenging for you to find joy in the Christian life?

Read ~:~ Reflect ~:~ Respond

~:~ Holiness is the work of God's grace in us and our response to God's call to live in Christ, seeking to think, act, feel, and live as Christ. Reflect on your own call to holiness with these passages: Matthew 5:17–45, John 13:34–35, Romans 6:22, 1 Corinthians 1:30, and *Catechism of the Catholic Church* 2012–2016, 2818–2820.

~:~ The Church's love for the poor is inspired by the Beatitudes and by Jesus' own concern for those who were in need. As you study these passages, think about the way the poor are treated in the world today: Psalm 34:6, Proverbs 19:17, Zechariah 7:8–10, Matthew 25:31–46, Luke 10:25–37, and *Catechism of the Catholic Church* 1807–1808, 2423–2424, 2443–2446.

Venerable Teresita Quevedo

Blessed are those who hunger and thirst for righteousness, for they will be filled (Matthew 5:6).

Teresita made the Blessed Virgin Mary the model and guide of her life. Through an abundance of small kindnesses and profound prayers, she offered Mary the gift of joyful service.

Discussion Questions

~::~ Teresita Quevedo's yearning for holiness could be summed up in her desire to honor the Mother of God. In this story there are multiple examples of her Marian devotion. Her love for Mary, more than a prayer or a statue, was a whole way of living, loving, and serving. How have you experienced this thirst for holiness in your own life? Which of the examples of Teresita's way of honoring Mary are helpful to you in strengthening your own pursuit of holiness?

~::~ To pursue holiness is to live according to God's will and to reflect God's glory in your life, in the big things and in the myriad seemingly insignificant moments that fill your day. How did you think about the small things in your own life before reading the example of Teresita? How do you think about them now?

~::~ Teresita was declared venerable by Saint John Paul II on June 9, 1983. During his pontificate, Pope Saint John Paul canonized 482 saints and beatified 1,338 because he wanted to raise up before the eyes of the Church the people on every continent and from every walk of life who had responded to the "universal call to holiness." Talk about a time when you responded to this call to holiness in your life. What was challenging for you? What have you learned from Teresita that would help you to strive for sanctity in your daily life?

~::~ Teresita's secret of holiness and pleasing Jesus was found in living with Mary, imitating her virtues, and sharing her intentions. Does the description of Teresita's Marian devotion resonate with your own? What was most enlightening for you? What was most challenging?

Read ~::~ Reflect ~::~ Respond

~::~ Prayer can permeate our lives and every moment of our day. This is one of the secrets of the Kingdom. Learn more about prayer in the following passages: 1 Chronicles 16:11, Jeremiah 33:3, John 15:16, 1 Thessalonians 5:17, Romans 8:26, and *Catechism of the Catholic Church* 2560–2561, 2660–2661.

~::~ Though we are already caught up in salvation through our Baptism, holiness is an ongoing process. We who are still sinners turn our eyes to Mary, model of holiness. Use these passages to deepen your love for Mary in your own life: Luke 1:26–38, John 2:2–11, Galatians 4:4–7, and *Catechism of the Catholic Church* 967–971, 975, 2030, 2679.

Saint Frances Xavier Cabrini

Blessed are the merciful, for they will receive mercy (Matthew 5:7).

Mother Cabrini made herself an immigrant among immigrants, embracing, as she said, "everything—labors, joys, and pains—for the salvation of all people."

Discussion Questions

~:~ The most Sacred Heart of Jesus is a deep sign and symbol of Jesus' love for all humanity, and each of us in particular. Frances Cabrini made this love of Jesus present to so many through her service to them. Have you thought about how your acts of service and attentiveness to others are also ways in which the love of Jesus becomes present in someone's life?

~:~ How did you understand the beatitude, "Blessed are the merciful," before reading this story? After learning about Frances Cabrini's heart for immigrants, the sick, and those who are suffering from economic and social marginalization, what aspect of that love for others speaks most to you?

~:~ Throughout the growth of her religious community, the Missionary Sisters of the Sacred Heart of Jesus, Frances Cabrini was led by God to care for people in ways she had not anticipated. Find one example of this in her story and talk about the way in which it opens your heart to a greater understanding of what God might be asking of you.

~:~ When Mother Cabrini was asked by Bishop Corrigan to begin a hospital for the poor, she declined because it was not part of the mission of her congregation. However, after a dream in which she understood Mary to be showing her that she was to include nursing as part of her apostolic work, she agreed to take on this project. Share the story of a new understanding, a surprising twist, or a deeper discernment which led you to take on a new project or ministry. How did you know it was something you were meant to do?

Read ~:~ Reflect ~:~ Respond

~:~ By loving us to the end, Jesus manifested to us the Father's love. We imitate the love of Jesus when we show love to one another. As you reflect on these passages, how might they be speaking to your own life? Psalm 112:5–9, Proverbs 19:17, Isaiah 58:7, Matthew 25:31–46, Luke 10:27–37, and *Catechism of the Catholic Church* 1822–1825, 2447–2448.

~:~ Jesus knew and loved each of us in his life and Passion with a human heart. The Sacred Heart of Jesus is considered an eloquent sign and symbol of that love with which he loves the Father and all human beings without exception. Pray with these passages: Matthew 11:28–30, Romans 5:5–8, 2 Corinthians 5:14–15, Ephesians 2:4–8, and *Catechism of the Catholic Church* 478–483, 1823.

Saint Martin de Porres

Blessed are the merciful, for they will receive mercy (Matthew 5:7).

He was known as "Martin the Charitable" because from his youth, his life was one continual act of gentle and generous service to others. Regardless of how he was treated, he saw Christ in everyone.

Discussion Questions

~:~ What stages or experiences of Martin's life resonate with your own? What about Martin's attitude toward life, prayer, or mercy toward others would be most helpful in reframing your own life experience?

~:~ The story of Martin de Porres illustrates the way a person grows dynamically in holiness, union with God through prayer, and participation in sharing Jesus' love with the world. Trace your own path of growth in holiness, prayer, and charity. What do you notice? What is most helpful in Martin's life in jumpstarting your own journey of discipleship?

~:~ When you re-read events recounted in the story of Martin de Porres, there is a sense of the newness of the Kingdom of God that is unmistakable. Describe how you have witnessed or personally experienced this newness yourself. Share the story of someone who, in your opinion, is longing for something more in life, for a joy that goes beyond the politics, values, and demands of this world. How would you explain to them the joy you have seen in the life of Martin de Porres?

~:~ There is a way in which Martin de Porres showed "mercy" and extended care to others all throughout his life, even when he himself was not being treated with mercy. Experiences which could have led to bitterness, through God's grace opened him up to understand the sufferings of others and to treat them mercifully. Do you think of yourself as a merciful person? What aspect of Martin's life would be most helpful for you to imitate?

Read ~:~ Reflect ~:~ Respond

~:~ Christians, who live with trust in the Father, bring about on this earth the newness of the Kingdom. As you reflect on these passages, ask for the grace to grow in trust: Hosea 12:6, Isaiah 30:18–19, Micah 6:8, Revelation 21:22–27, and *Catechism of the Catholic Church* 2818–2821, 2828–2837.

~:~ All Christians are called to fullness of life in Christ. There is no limit to the holiness and the intimate union with God that we can attain. Explore the call to holiness in these passages: Jeremiah 33:3, Matthew 6:5–8, Luke 18:1–8, 1 Thessalonians 5:16–18, Hebrews 12:14, and *Catechism of the Catholic Church* 2013–2016, 2659–2660.

Saint Kateri Tekakwitha

Blessed are the pure in heart, for they will see God (Matthew 5:8).

Known as the "glory of the Mohawks," this young Native North American was divinely inspired to seek out instructions in the Catholic faith, be baptized, and live as a virgin for Christ.

Discussion Questions

~::~ The pure of heart will see God in heaven face to face and be like him. On this earth, purity of heart enables us to see others the way God sees them and to accept them as our sisters and brothers. Those who are pure of heart perceive their body, and that of others, as a temple of the Holy Spirit. Can you identify the ways in which Kateri grew in purity of heart throughout her life? Which aspects of Kateri's behavior, attitudes, and spirit are most attractive to you? Which are the most challenging?

~::~ Kateri was intentional about pursuing what she wanted in life. She had a pure vision about who she was and what was truly important. Have you experienced times when you had to make critical decisions in order to live your faith with integrity? What made it easier to do so? What can you learn from the strength, determination, and courage of Kateri?

~::~ The *Catechism of the Catholic Church* states that purity of heart has to do with attuning ourselves to the demands of God's holiness in three areas of our life: "charity; chastity or sexual rectitude; love of truth and orthodoxy of faith"

(CCC 2518). Throughout her life, Kateri Tekakwitha sought to grow in understanding the truth, in charity and service of others, and in chastity. As you look over her story, can you find examples for each of these areas of her life in which she attuned herself to God's holiness? Talk about what it would mean to grow in purity of heart in one of these areas of your own life.

~::~ We shape our lives through the exercise of our free will. Kateri was remarkably mature in her free response to the invitations of grace throughout her life. What impressed you about the habits and virtues she practiced, which strengthened her exercise of freedom and made her more docile to the promptings of divine grace?

Read ~::~ Reflect ~::~ Respond

~::~ Purity of heart, Jesus tells us in the beatitude, will enable us to see God. It also purifies our vision and inspires a way of life renewed by the Gospel so that our whole life is restored in Christ. Let these readings help you reflect on your own purity of heart: Psalm 24:3–10, Romans 12:1, Colossians 3:1–3, 1 Peter 1:15–26, Revelation 14:1–4, and *Catechism of the Catholic Church* 2349, 2518–2520.

~::~ The tension or struggle that the human person experiences within themselves to live by the Spirit is a part of the daily effort needed in the spiritual battle for holiness. Read these passages to reflect on your own daily battle to follow Christ: Romans 7:14–25, 1 Corinthians 6:18–20, Ephesians 5:1–20, James 1:13–21, and *Catechism of the Catholic Church* 1741–1742, 2514–2519.

Blessed Marie-Clémentine
Anuarite Nengapeta

Blessed are the pure in heart, for they will see God (Matthew 5:8).

As a young religious, when she was called upon to face the ultimate test of virtue with little time to prepare, Anuarite chose to stand firm and accept death rather than sin. She witnessed to her commitment with her life.

Discussion Questions

~::~ In this story, Anuarite's inner beauty and kindness are demonstrated in a number of ways. Do her attentive, giving, tender, and patient actions speak to any struggles you may have? How did her daily choices lead to her strength of character?

~::~ Reflect on the difference between Anuarite and the rebels who attempted to seduce her to become Colonel Ngalo's wife. How would you describe their different visions of the human person? Of God? Of love?

~::~ What do you think enabled Anuarite to handle the situation that led to her martyrdom the way she did? Would you have done the same? Why or why not?

~::~ The description in the story of Anuarite's struggles in the spiritual battle for holiness reminds us that all saints were human beings who, like us, had to make daily choices to live by the Spirit and who sometimes struggled with their character and fell short of what God was asking of them. How did Anuarite handle her weaknesses and

mistakes? How would you describe your own daily journey to follow Christ? Is there an image or a song or a
word that characterizes it best? How do you experience
the presence of God with you on the way?

Read ~::~ Reflect ~::~Respond

~::~ "Chastity is a moral virtue. It is also a gift from God, a
grace, a fruit of spiritual effort" (CCC 2345). In keeping
with their own state in life, all the baptized are called
to chastity. Read these passages and reflect on your
own growth in the virtue of chastity: Matthew 6:23,
Romans 13:11–14, Philippians 4:8, 1 Thessalonians
5:1–10, Hebrews 12:1–4, and *Catechism of the Catholic
Church* 2331–2332, 2337–2345.

~::~ As Christians we have been rescued from the power
of darkness and brought into the Lord's glorious light.
Through the gift of grace, we share in God's own nature.
Reflect on your daily choices and how they contribute
to your interior growth toward the perfection of charity:
Proverbs 16:2, Isaiah 9:2, John 1:12, Romans 6:11–23,
Ephesians 1:3–14, and *Catechism of the Catholic Church*
1691–1696, 1700.

Saint Elizabeth of Hungary

Blessed are the peacemakers, for they will be called children of God (Matthew 5:9).

This young woman, wife and widow of the ruling count of Thuringia, and mother of three small children was a woman of peace. Her home was a haven of peace; she sought peace with her in-laws, in serving the needs of the poor, and in doing the will of God.

Discussion Questions

~:~ In the life of Elizabeth of Hungary, her relationship with her husband and love for her family was tied closely to her role in society as the landgravine of Thuringia. Family life is the smallest cell of society and the place where its members first learn how to love others and give to those who are in need. Does the family life of Elizabeth attract you? What are characteristics of a strong family life today that would contribute to the well-being of society?

~:~ "The vocation of humanity is to show forth the image of God and to be transformed into the image of the Father's only Son" (CCC 1877). Before reading the life of Elizabeth, had you ever thought about your vocation as a calling to reveal the image of God to the world? How did Elizabeth of Hungary do this? Can you identify two or three personal qualities that show forth the image of God to others?

~:~ In human communities, the dignity of persons requires that we be concerned for justice and charity. Elizabeth did this in two ways. Though other members of the royalty gave of their wealth to care for the sick and the marginalized, Elizabeth of Hungary went personally to be with them and to provide for them the structures and the services that they needed to survive. Also, she and her husband built a married relationship that was strong, loyal, and loving even though fidelity was uncommon in the courtly circles of that time. What parts of Elizabeth's story resonated with you? What were the most difficult or challenging aspects of her life for you personally?

~:~ Even after all the work Elizabeth had undertaken to provide for the desperately poor people of her land, when she was thrown out of the castle, no one came to her assistance and she walked the streets, begging for scraps of food. In both wealth and poverty, she responded with love. Talk about a time when you were treated unjustly. Has reading about the life of Elizabeth given you insight into how love can be the foundation for every season of your life?

Read ~:~ Reflect ~:~ Respond

~:~ Social changes that truly serve the human person are brought about by inner conversion and charity, which lead us to respect others and their rights, practice justice, and live a life of self-giving. Read these passages and ask the Holy Spirit to guide you to the interior conversion in your own life that will contribute to social change in the world: Isaiah 1:17, Zechariah 7:9–10, Jeremiah 22:3, Matthew 25:31–46, Romans 12:15–18, and *Catechism of the Catholic Church* 1877–1879, 1888.

~:~ Elizabeth put the well-being of her family—husband and children—first. The family is the domestic church and the original cell of social life. "Authority, stability, and a life of relationships within the family constitute the foundations for freedom, security, and fraternity within society" (CCC 2207). Explore the important relationship between the family and society: Genesis 2:24, Deuteronomy 6:6–7, Romans 12:9–21, Ephesians 2:15–17, 1 John 4:7, and *Catechism of the Catholic Church* 2204–2211.

Saint Catherine of Siena

Blessed are the peacemakers, for they will be called children of God (Matthew 5:9).

Patron saint of Italy and Doctor of the Church, Catherine of Siena was a mystic and true apostle of peace. In her thirty-three years of life, she and her followers brought about a great renewal in the Church.

Discussion Questions

~:~ Catherine of Siena, while still in her twenties, was called to a more public life. She established correspondence with influential figures, advising popes and political figures in her efforts to unify the Church and bring peace to Italy, which was in political turmoil at that time. As a peacemaker she promoted and embraced humility, patience, justice, a willingness to listen, and a desire to promote unity and bring about reconciliation. Can you identify these or other peacemaking qualities in the story of Catherine of Siena? Do you think of yourself as a peacemaker? Is there a situation in your life that needs the gift of peace?

~:~ Catherine spent several years exclusively in prayer and family service. After that, Jesus sent her into the world as his ambassador of peace, restoring relationships and working to bring about harmony where there was strife. What are some clues in the story that she continued to find her strength and direction in prayer? Have you ever thought of prayer as the source of courage and direction in your life?

~:~ Catherine of Siena remained deeply faithful to God, which allowed her to be an effective and influential woman of peace and healing, sought after by city officials to resolve conflicts and bring about reconciliation. She supported the unity of the Church but also called for reform when necessary. Talk about the challenges she would have faced building bridges in the fourteenth century as a woman, as a lay Catholic, as a young adult. Do some of these challenges still exist today? What can we learn from Catherine's example?

~:~ Catherine had many disciples who followed her as she went about her mission. In her prayers and letters, she taught them about prayer, for she believed that it was prayer that widened her vision, deepened her wisdom, and strengthened her work to build peace. Describe a time when prayer was the key factor that made the difference for you in living your vocation.

Read ~:~ Reflect ~:~Respond

~:~ Saint Catherine of Siena in her prayer called the most precious Blood of Christ an ocean of Divine Mercy. In the *Catechism*, the Church states that by his blood, Jesus reconciled all people with God and "made his Church the sacrament of the unity of the human race and of its union with God" (CCC 2305). Learn more about how the Father has "willed to call the whole of humanity together into his Son's Church" (CCC 845): Matthew 26:28, Colossians 1:13–14, Hebrews 9:14, 1 John 1:7, Revelation 1:5, and *Catechism of the Catholic Church* 813, 836-838, 845, 2304–2306.

~:~ Prayer is where God's thirst for us meets our thirst for him. In prayer we find that God himself sustains our efforts for making peace and bringing about reform. Reflect on these passages to deepen your thirst for God: Psalm 63:1, Judges 15:18–19, Nehemiah 9:15, Isaiah 48:21, John 4:1–42, and *Catechism of the Catholic Church* 2559–2561, 2626–2639.

Blessed Isidore Bakanja

Blessed are those who are persecuted for righteousness'
sake, for theirs is the kingdom of heaven
(Matthew 5:10).

At his death, Isidore was a young man and a recent convert intent on bettering himself in a new occupation. Because of his desire to witness to his faith and strong devotion to Mary, which he showed by wearing a scapular, he was persecuted and killed.

Discussion Questions

~:~ John Paul II said in his homily at the beatification of Isidore Bakanja that on the African continent, catechists are indispensable to supporting the work of the priest in ministering to the faithful. During periods of persecution, it was the ministry and the suffering of catechists that enabled the faith to survive. Isidore had been a Catholic for only three years by the time the events of this story took place. He wasn't trained as a catechist yet had a clear idea of his responsibility as a baptized Christian. How do you understand the purpose of your life as a member of the Church?

~:~ As you prayerfully read once again the moments of his self-reflection, struggle, and prayer before determining how to live his faith in this particular situation, what stands out to you? What is the most illuminating? What is the most challenging?

~:~ Isidore knew that his brothers and sisters were eager to hear the proclamation of the Good News and the joyous revelation of God's love for us. He witnessed to Christ, the Good Shepherd, in making choices that would clearly witness to the faith so that others would find Christ. You are in the same situation as Isidore. You are surrounded by people who, without your testimony, may never know the love of Jesus. Upon hearing this, what is your initial reaction? How can you bring this reaction to prayer?

~::~ Isidore believed in his own dignity as a human person and the dignity of others. He was willing to stand up to his oppressive boss on behalf of all his people, affirming their human rights, even the right to practice their faith. What are the most challenging or difficult parts of Isidore's story for you personally? What are the most enlightening or encouraging?

Read ~::~ Reflect ~::~ Respond

~::~ By virtue of their Baptism and Confirmation, lay Catholics have the right and duty to proclaim the message of salvation so it may be known by all people. Each of us with our respective gifts are sent by Christ to the people we encounter so that they, too, might know the love that Jesus has for them. Use these passages to reflect on your gifts that may contribute to the Church's proclamation of the message of the Gospel: Psalm 105:1, Matthew 5:15–16, John 3:16–17, Acts 1:8, 2 Timothy 1:8–9, and *Catechism of the Catholic Church* 422–429, 900–901, 905.

~::~ A martyr gives the supreme witness to the truth of the faith even unto death. As you explore the scriptural and theological meaning of martyrdom, reflect on how you can more fully live your own faith with these readings: Isaiah 53:7, Mark 13:9–13, Luke 21:16–17, Hebrews 12:2–15, Revelation 6:9–11, and *Catechism of the Catholic Church* 2472–2474.

Saint Mary MacKillop
(Mother Mary of the Cross)

Blessed are those who are persecuted for righteousness' sake, for theirs is the kingdom of heaven (Matthew 5:10).

The first canonized saint of Australia, Mary engaged all her love and energies in the work of education and catechesis, serving the needy, and advocating for prisoners and oppressed laborers. She overcame all odds, including harassment and accusation, by her living devotion to the Sacred Heart.

Discussion Questions

~:~ Mother Mary MacKillop's life story demonstrates both the complexity and the simplicity of accomplishing the mission for which we were created. What elements of her experience as a foundress were confusing, unfair, or mishandled? Talk about the clarity and courage with which Mother Mary met these situations. Have you watched movies or read books about other saints who have lived through similar situations?

~:~ Many of the situations described in this story of Mary MacKillop resonate with us in the Church today. As you were reading the story, what were you feeling? Can you talk to God about what this story brought up for you? What of Mother Mary's spirituality speaks to you most strongly?

~:~ Mother Mary wrote to her sisters near the end of her life: "Let our life together be like a bit of heaven on earth. No matter what swirls around outside, no matter the humiliations and sufferings, among us there should be only love and charity." This is difficult to live in practice. Do you think it was easy for Mother Mary? Do you think that in her life she grew in her ability to love and to remain in peace no matter what "was swirling around outside"? What do you think would have helped her keep going in the darkest days?

~::~ Do you know someone directly impacted by abuse in the Church? What are some ways that you could support someone who has been the victim of abuse? When Mother Mary reported a priest who had abused children in her school, she ended up paying a very big price. Talk about ways that people may suffer for their willingness to seek justice for those who have been victimized. What have you learned in Mother Mary MacKillop's story that would be helpful to you?

Read ~::~ Reflect ~::~ Respond

~::~ The Lord spoke often of forgiveness, even to the forgiveness of enemies. This forgiveness that imitates Jesus who loved us to the end configures the disciple to the Master. As you reflect upon these passages, ask for the grace to extend forgiveness to anyone who has hurt you: Isaiah 43:25, Psalm 86:5, Matthew 6:14, Luke 6:37, Ephesians 4:32, Colossians 3:13, and *Catechism of the Catholic Church* 2838–2845.

~::~ "United with Christ, the Church is sanctified by him; through him and with him she becomes sanctifying" (CCC 824). The Church is holy and yet ever in need of purification, for each of her members is a sinner. In the Church are both weeds and wheat, for all are still on the way to holiness. Read more about the Church's call to holiness: Matthew 9:11–13, 1 Corinthians 5:6–8, Ephesians 5:25–27, 1 Timothy 1:12–17, 2 Timothy 1:8-9, Revelation 19:7–8, and *Catechism of the Catholic Church* 823–829.

Alphabetical Listing of Saints

Marie Paul Curley, FSP

As a child, the stories of the saints captured Sister Marie Paul Curley's imagination. Her early fascination has continued throughout her religious life as a Daughter of St. Paul. She has written and produced numerous Catholic television programs on the saints for both children and adults. She currently serves as an acquisition editor for Pauline Books & Media. You can find Sister Marie Paul online by visiting: www.pauline.org/mariepaulcurley.

Mary Lea Hill, FSP

Sister Mary Lea Hill, a member of the Daughters of St. Paul since 1964, has enjoyed communicating the faith through a variety of apostolic assignments. Her skills as a story-teller were honed as director of audiovisual productions when Pauline Books and Media first produced animated features in the early 80s. An editor and author for many years, Sister Mary Lea has written a number of books, including *Growing in Virtue, One Vice at a Time: With a Crabby Mystic; Complaints of the Saints; Blessed Are the Stressed*; and the best-selling *Basic Catechism* (co-authored with Sister Susan Helen Wallace). Sister Mary Lea can be found on Instagram or Facebook as @crabbymystic.

Thank You.

Your purchase of this book and engagement with our other projects supports us in the work we do as Daughters of St. Paul. This book is the fruit of our consecrated life, prayer, and mission of communicating God's love.

We hold you and all your intentions in our prayers. We invite you to connect with us or send us prayer intentions at pauline.org.

Pauline
BOOKS & MEDIA